TALKING PICTURES
The Popular
Experience of the Cinema

Edited by
Colin Harding
&
Brian Lewis

Everyone has a story
to tell. We find
ways of helping
them tell it.

NATIONAL MUSEUM
PHOTOGRAPHY • FILM • TELEVISION

PICTUREVILLE • BRADFORD

1993

Published jointly by Yorkshire Art Circus, School Lane
Castleford WF10 4QH, and the National Museum of
Photography, Film & Television, Pictureville, Bradford
BD1 1NQ

Distributed by Yorkshire Art Circus, Glasshoughton Cultural
Industries School Lane, Castleford WF10 4QH
© Text - Yorkshire Art Circus and the National Museum of
    Photography, Film & Television
© Photographs - National Museum of Photography,
    Film & Television and contributors
© Commissioned photographs - Stephen McClarence

Editorial and Research Team:
Pam Davenport, Steve Davenport,
Olive Fowler, Tony Lumb,
Margaret Morton, Margaret Pilkington,
Reini Schühle.

Design and Technical Team:
Adele Broadley, Bob Cox, Jane Crumack,
Paul Thompson

Printed by:
Thornton and Pearson Ltd., Rosse Street, Thornton Road
Bradford BD8 9AS

Typesetting by:
Mousehouse, Hornbeam Park, Harrogate HG2 8QT

ISBN 0 947780 90 4

Classification: Film/General Interest

Yorkshire Art Circus is supported by:
Yorkshire and Humberside Arts
West Yorkshire Grants
Wakefield MDC

The NMPFT is part of the National Museum of Science &
Industry
IMAX® is the registered trade mark of IMAX Systems
Corporation, Toronto, Canada

FOREWORD

Yorkshire Art Circus is a unique book publisher,
bringing to all members of its community the opportunity
to write about their lives and experiences, and to put them in print.
The National Museum of Photography, Film and Television is a unique museum,
interpreting for everyone the media which form part of all our lives.
With such complementary aims, it is almost inevitable -
and entirely logical - that these two Yorkshire institutions
should become partners .

Last year we looked at the popular
experience of photography and, by getting people to write and talk
about their family photographs, produced Kept In A Shoebox,
a prize-winner in the prestigious Raymond Williams community
publishing competition organised by the Arts Council.
This year, we have turned our attention to cinema-going.

The book started with Yorkshire Art Circus
interviewing in the Museum, in schools, workplaces, community
centres; in fact, anywhere where people congregated, and asking them
to talk about their experiences of visiting the cinema. We were not interested in
their opinion of individual film stars or in the critical evaluation of particular
films but in what the cinema meant to them.

Colin Ford, National Museum of Photography, Film & Television
Brian Lewis, Yorkshire Art Circus

INTRODUCTION

Like many of my generation - I am a child of the fifties - I owe a great personal debt to the cinema. It was in the back row of the Gnoll Road Cinema in Neath that my parents began the courtship that was to lead to their marriage and, later, my birth. That first date, to see *Murders in the Rue Morgue*, was not an outstanding success. Unbeknown to my father, my mother had settled herself comfortably on his brand new slouch hat. By the end of the evening, moulded by the weight and warmth of her body, it resembled the illegitimate offspring of chance liaison between a frisbee and a cowpat. Through gritted teeth he forgave her and invited her out again. Where to? - to the pictures, where else?

My parents' experience is of course by no means unusual. As they sat in shared darkness, they were simply doing the same as millions of other couples have done before and since. Yet the Cinema is not just for courting couples, it is for everyone. The Cinema offers us far more than merely a suitable venue to watch a film -it is an event, an *experience*. As Roger Manvell observed in his influential book *Film*, published in 1944 : 'There is more to cinema-going than seeing films. There is going out at night, the sense of relaxation combined with the sense of fun and excitement.' It was this sense of fun and excitement that proved to be too much for some self-appointed guardians of our morals. What possible good, they argued, could come from any form of entertainment which involved people sitting in darkness, surrounded by total strangers, watching scenes of lust and violence being played out before them. Here we have one of the essential contradictions of cinema-going. It is a public, shared experience but it is also an essentially private one. Cocooned in intimate darkness, we view the film in our own private world and then share our experience with others. 'What did you think of the film, then?'

It is nearly one hundred years since the first public film show took place in Britain, on 20 February, 1896. Moving pictures soon spread throughout the country, linked to other forms of popular entertainment such as the circus and fairground. Theatres and music halls showed films

and soon, the first purpose-built cinemas began to appear. A distinct change in the social acceptance of the Cinema occurred. At first, very much a working-class form of entertainment, the Cinema started to appeal to a much broader and sophisticated audience. By the time of the First World War a visit to a picture palace had become a normal activity. It was in the years immediately following the Second World War that Cinema was to enjoy its period of greatest popularity. In 1946, the peak year for British cinema-going, weekly audiences exceeded thirty million and there were nearly five thousand cinemas. During the 1950s, however, with the growth of television, cinema attendances began to decline dramatically. In 1960 under ten million people went to he cinema each week and by 1984 weekly audiences had reached an all-time low of just one million. Recently, the Cinema has begun to show signs of a slight revival. It is very unlikely, however, that its popularity will ever return to the levels that it enjoyed during the thirties and forties - the Golden Age of Cinema.

Many histories of the cinema have been written. Most of them, however, concentrate on the technological, aesthetic or economic aspects of film history or on the work of particular individuals or studios. The social history of the cinema is a comparatively neglected area and the study of cinema audiences has been barely touched upon. And yet, some understanding of the nature of the cinema audience is surely fundamental if we are to have any chance of making sense of how and why films work in the way that they do. The history of cinema involves four elements - a technology, an aesthetic, an economy and an *audience*. Each of these elements are inter-related and each of them is equally important. In this book we approach the history of the cinema from the point of view of the audience and those who worked in the cinema. What we mean by the popular experience of the cinema.

Colin Harding
National Museum of Photography,
Film & Television

We should like to thank the following people for sharing their stories and photographs:

Stephen Abbey, Linda Allan, Judi Alston, Lesley Andrews, Mr Andrews, Paul Archer, Mr Armstrong, Lesley Atkinson, Margaret Bagg, Gwen Baines, Joan Bates, Matthew Bateman, Paul Bedford, Gillian Beeham, Mrs J Beecham, Catherine Bentley, Janine Birch, Stephen Blythe, Charlie Bool, Dorothy Bool, Keith Bowen, Colin Bright, Christina Broom, Gill Brown, Bob Brown, Pauline Burgin, Bernard Carley, Sharon C.K. Caswell, Liza Chambers, Shirley Champla Kumar, Catherine Clark, Michael Clark, Stanley Claughton, Ian Clayton, Mrs Annie Cliff, Pauline Costello, Ian Daley, Nancy Daley, Tina Davies, James Dearie, Chris Donaghy, Bernard Dore, Rosalyn Edwards, Cyril Edwards, Ekaette Ekong, Arthur Ellis, James Faulkner, J Fitzgerald, John Foakes, Geoff Ford, Olive Fowler, David Francis, Isabel Galan, Jane Goodwin, Joan Gordon, Katherine Hague, Joyce Harding, Doug Harding, Sheilagh Harrison, Bob Hayhurst, Chris Heinitz, Mary Hobson, M Hodson, Mrs Holmes, Anthony Hopkins, Viv Hughes, Christine Hulme, Gordon Jackson, Clare Jenkins, William Jevons, David Alan Jones, Don Jones, Ken Jones, Susan Jones, Patricia Joyce, Jenny Kaye, Carole Kenyon, K M Kerr-Morgan, Shirley Julie Lawler, Tom Leek, Nora Leese, Steven Leigh, Ernest Lewis, John Lewis, G Linaker, Liz Lloyd, Alf Lloyd, Malcolm Lock, Gloria Lock, Tony Lumb, Deidre Lynsky, Deirdre MacDonogh, Steve McClarence, Harry Malkin, Pat Mantle, Don Marquis, Jean Marquis, Derek Mills, Maxine Mills, Linda Maynard, Dorothy Montague, Christine Moorsby, Ken Morgan, Rita Morley, Robert Munn, Jack Nalton, Lily Need, Marjorie Oldfield, Linda Oats, Winifred O'Rourke, Liz Outing, Pamela Pennock, Alan Pilkington, Margaret Pilkington, M W Radcliffe, Norman Ratcliffe, Joy Rathbone, Stephen Rayworth, Rene Reynolds, T Robinson, Tom Robinson, John Ross, Mike Savage, Reini Schühle, Josephine Scholey, John Scwires, Annette Sharman, Nibadita Sen, Peter Shields, Margaret Shooter, Brian Siberry, Clifford Shaw, Mohamoud Shirwan, Vanessa Sionneau, Jean Skenfield, Stuart Smith, Alan Stephens, Mary Stott, Elsie Sykes, V Szewc, Mohammed Tariq, Martin Tarpey, Patrick Tawney, Gerry Temple, Joyce Temple, Mrs Temple, Judith Tingay, Peter Thomas, Sheila Thorpe, Gaynor Thorpe, Julie Tunnacliffe, Fred Turley, Steve Turnbull, Anna Twaddell, Diane Varley, Vasilis Vasiliou, Uli Verspohl, Verena Verspohl, Gerald David Wagstaff, Carl Wain, Alf Walker, M Walters, Franz Weiller, Tracy White, Lillian Whiteley, Dave Wilders, Amanda Wilson, Mick Wilson, Louise Winfield, Frances Wingate, Elizabeth Wood, Jerry Woodgate, Enola Wright, Olive Yates, Margaret Zadorozny.

Special thanks to Bob Preedy, author of *Leeds Cinemas* and Geoff Mellor, author of *Cinemas of Bradford*

CHAPTER ONE

THE
GREAT ILLUSION

SHADOW PUPPETS

Shadow plays, the oldest form of moving pictures on a screen, have taken place in the Far East for thousands of years. The puppets are cut-out figures supported by thin rods. The puppet operators speak dialogue and the performance is accompanied by music.

THE MAGIC LANTERN

Magic lanterns first appeared in the seventeenth century. Using candles or oil lamps, these early lanterns produced only small, dimly lit pictures. During the last century however, with the discovery of new illuminants such as limelight, the magic lantern was transformed from a curiosity into a source of popular entertainment. With multiple lens lanterns it was possible to create a range of dramatic special effects.

THE ZOETROPE

The idea that a sequence of drawings, when viewed in a rotating, slotted cylinder, would produce the illusion of movement, was first suggested in 1833. The zoetrope was just one of a number of popular Victorian optical toys with equally exotic names such as the praxinoscope and the phenakistoscope.

LE PRINCE CAMERA

Louis Le Prince was born in France but lived in Leeds. Reputedly, in 1888, using this camera he succeeded in taking moving pictures of traffic crossing Leeds bridge. His pioneering film work came to an abrupt end in September 1890, when, after being seen boarding a train for Paris at Dijon, he disappeared, never to be seen again.

THE KINETOSCOPE

The kinetoscope was a film viewer designed in 1893 by W.K.L Dickson, Thomas Alva Edison's assistant. A floor-standing wooden box, it contained about fifty feet of film running in an endless loop. Only person could view at a time. In April 1894 the first kinetoscope parlour was opened to the public. By the end of the year there were parlours all over North America and Europe, including one in London.

THE CINEMATOGRAPHE

Invented by the Lumière brothers, Auguste and Louis, the Cinématographe was a combined film camera and projector. Using the Cinématographe the brothers gave the first ever public film performance to a paying audience, in Paris on 28 December, 1895.

KINEMACOLOR PROJECTOR

The first 'natural colour' film process, Kinemacolor was developed by George Albert Smith and Charles Urban. Alternate frames were shot on black and white film through red and green filters. When projected through a similar filter wheel mounted on the front of the projector this gave the illusion of colour. Kinemacolor films were made of the Coronation procession of King George V in 1911 and the Delhi Durbar of 1912.

ROSS VITAPHONE PROJECTOR

Introduced by Warner Brothers early in 1926, Vitaphone was a sound-on-disc system in which the film sound was recorded onto sixteen inch diameter gramophone records. Special projectors were needed to synchronise the soundtrack with the film. *The Jazz Singer,* made in 1927 and probably the most famous of all the early talkies, was made using the Vitaphone system.

TECHNICOLOR CAMERA

Technicolor was the standard colour motion picture process for many years.. The camera exposed three strips of film, individually sensitive to red, green and blue light. The resulting negatives were combined at the printing stage. Technicolor was popular until the 1950s and was used to shoot some classic films such as *Gone with the Wind*.

IMAX PROJECTOR

The Imax system uses the world's largest film format, with 70mm film running horizontally through the projector. The large frame size (ten times that of 35mm film) allows projection of startling size and clarity. Britain's only Imax projector is at the National Museum of Photography, Film & Television where it uses the country's biggest cinema screen - five storeys high.

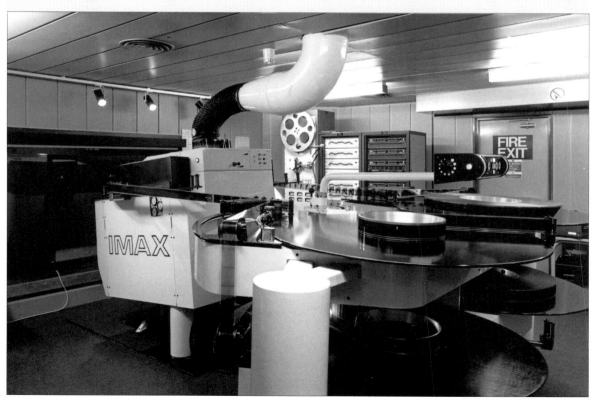

If you are on a blind date and
he's ugly there's no better place to go
than the cinema.

CHAPTER TWO

THE CINEMA
WILL NEVER DIE
AS LONG AS THERE ARE
COURTING COUPLES

From being about thirteen, going to the pictures was the only real social life I had. Being too young to go in the pubs - they really did chuck you out in those days - and too sophisticated, as I saw it, for the youth clubs, there was no alternative except hang about on the street corners. I used to go to the pictures with my bosom friend, Mavis, who lived in the same street as me and whose strict parents only allowed her out on the understanding that we would go to the first house at the Pav at Wombwell. We weren't supposed to talk to lads and promised solemnly that we would not. We got five bob pocket money and it covered our bus fares, ten Gold Leaf, the odd box of matches - which I got to keep since her mother searched her handbag - a packet of chewing gum or Polos to kill the smell and our tickets into the front stalls. This budget was so tight that it was nearly scuppered when the front stalls seats went up to 3d, and we had to change to a cheaper brand of cigs. We always sat in the same seats with the same crowd of adolescents and generally made a nuisance of ourselves. We must have seen all the very worst B movies of the late fifties and early sixties. Occasionally we got chucked out and had to kill the time until the quarter past nine number seventy bus home either by walking up and down the High Street or gatecrashing the church youth club.

My first date at the pictures was with Carol Fley when I was ten. We went to the Saturday morning rush at the ABC. After half an hour just sitting together I plucked up the courage to reach for her hand. To my relief she took my hand and threw me a smile that would have melted the heart of a statue. I can still recall that feeling. In love and every nerve tingling, it was heaven. Alone on the way home I marvelled at the newness of it all but although I sensed wonder I was also puzzled.

'Mum', I said when I got in. 'Why did my pinkle go all hard when I held Carol's hand?' I can't remember what she said but the answer didn't satisfy me.

You would sit down for a while and then all of a sudden you would hear shuffling noises behind you. A likely lad was trying to attract your attention. If you liked him you were away, if not, you moved your seat. There was so much moving about that I don't think we ever saw a full film. That's unless it was Elvis and then God himself could sit behind you and you wouldn't notice.

I was twelve and Sundays were always boring. If my friends were out I'd mooch round the house complaining. One Sunday my parents had had enough of me and suggested I go to the cinema. Brilliant. I was a grown - up going on my own. I dressed myself up feeling wonderful and my dad ran me there. It was *The Greatest Story Ever Told*. The cinema looked amazing and I really felt I'd arrived.

After about ten minutes a bloke came and sat next to me. He leaned my way so I edged away from him. He seemed to lean even further. Was it my imagination or was he really doing it? I summoned up all my courage and moved nearer to other people. Relief - although I still felt a bit scared. It wasn't over. He then came and sat next to me again. I was terrified. Should I get up and leave? What would I say to my parents? Where would I go? Would he follow me? I decided to wait and at least leave with other people. I was really scared, more so than I think I've ever felt since. He gradually put his arm around me. I felt helpless and quite unable to respond. The film was not a long one but it seemed to go on forever. Eventually it did end and I left with a crowd but he followed me. I answered his questions in monosyllables as I walked to the bus stop. I was never more relieved than when the number seventy-three bus arrived. He wanted to get on the bus but I promised to meet him the next day. I never said a word to my parents, I was too shaken. The next day I told my friends but not about the fear, just about meeting a bloke at the cinema. He was handsome and old - almost eighteen - and he'd asked me out. I was too frightened to tell them about the feeling of helplessness.

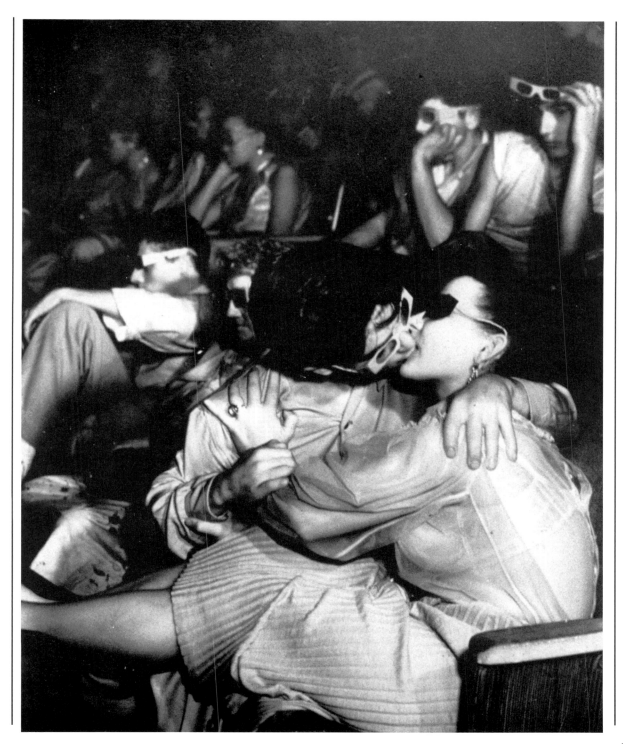

❧ I was as green as they come. George from the weaving shed offered to take me. He even paid for my ticket.

The film started. His arm came around my shoulders to comfort me from the dreaded monster. I was soon to realise that the real monster was George. He lost no time at all in trying to unbutton my blouse. His hands were eveywhere.

I writhed and twisted. His hands moved from my knees to my boobs.

Trapped between two other couples, unlike me enjoying the groping, I had nowhere to go but under the seat in front of me. I gradually slithered down until neither him nor me could do anything but wait for the lights to come up and escape.

❧ The first time I went to the cinema as a so-called adult I was fifteen years old. I had dressed with care because this was my first date.

The film was *Bonnie and Clyde* showing at the Clock Cinema, Roundhay Road in Leeds. I found the film very exciting until my date put his arm around me. From that moment I don't remember the film.

I had accepted the date, looking forward to going out on my first date and expecting my first kiss. The kiss happened. I was really looking forward to it and it had been the topic all day with my school mates. Being a romantic, I expected it to be beautiful with orchestras playing. But everything fell flat. To start with he had bad breath. He kissed me so hard it hurt my lips and before I could take a breath his hand was straight up my skirt. I tried not to panic but fighting him off was horrible. I worked myself into such a state that I cried and wet my knickers. He soon let go. Then he stood up, laughed at me and walked out. I sat there trembling. It took me ages to get up and go home. I felt everyone was looking at me. I was bedraggled and my clothes were wet.

It took ages to get over it, and even longer before I went to the cinema again. I felt the cinema to be an isolated place where help just wasn't available.

❧ I was fifteen and a boy about whom I was crazy asked me out. I was on cloud nine when I met him outside. Not surprisingly I can't remember the name of the film because from the moment he sat down he put his arm around me and started to kiss me. Then his hands started creeping all over me and I was very frightened. It was my first date and I thought at the time that it would be my last. I couldn't wait for the film to end because I was afraid to get up and walk out and afraid to make a fuss because it was so quiet in there.

I had liked this boy, who was about three or four years older than me, for a long time and couldn't believe that in such a short space of time I could change my opinion of someone so completely.

❧ One of the girls in our gang saw herself as the guardian of our morals, the keeper-in-check of the lad-mad ones of our number. Well, imagine our shock one night in the Ritz when after a gang of lads had sat at the back of us, bantering and chatting us up, much to her disaproval, we glanced along the line to see one lad's hand slipped inside her coat cradling her breast. The look on her face was totally inscrutable. Boy, did we give her some stick after that.

❧ Trying to undo someone's bra is never that easy, especially when it's your first attempt. A darkened cinema with *Jaws* being shown was responsible for my first experience. The tension of the music and the atmosphere in the auditorium made my hands even more shaky than they would normally have been. When I eventually succeeded in releasing the offending obstruction the girl giggled and pushed me playfully off. *Jaws* has never been the same since.

❧ The Bug House was a cheap night out but on Saturdays they would make the boys sit on one side and the girls on the opposite side of the aisle. The usherette would shine her torch on anyone who was silly enough to try to change sides. If the ice cream sales were not going well the manager used to turn up the heating.

❧ On the Greek island of Aegina there are two open air cinemas. We went about five times while on holiday. It was a lovely feeling to sit out in the open watching films, drinking cold beer with a man's arm around your waist and your skin tingling from the day's sun. The film I enjoyed most was *Throw Momma From The Train*, mainly because the subtitles were projected slap bang in the middle of the screen.

At one end Princes Street in Edinburgh deteriorates and becomes Leith Walk. One afternoon, when I was a student, I went there to relax and watch a film and get away from it all.

The auditorium was almost empty but as I sat there, a man who had been sitting two rows in front of me got up and came and sat near me. He had a raincoat over his arm and his hand was moving under the raincoat.

'I think that you had better move,' I said. Thankfully, he did.

That night, as I was undressing, I noticed something strange about my underskirt. A four-inch square had been cut out of the hem. I suspect that I wasn't his first victim - this was a practiced hand - but I often wonder what he did with the pieces.

The first time I was touched by one of those sleazy men was at the picture house in Filey. I was so shocked and disgusted I didn't say anything but just walked out and sobbed the sordid tale out to my mum when I got home.

'Always take a hat pin with you in future,' was her advice.

Blow me if I wasn't sat in there a couple of weeks later when it happened again with another bloke. I took out the hat pin and rammed it into the back of his hand. The yell he let out was very satisfying.

After my father retired, one of his chief pleasures was going to the matinees when it was cheap for pensioners. One day he came home looking very old and ill. I asked him what was wrong but he just sat down in his chair staring at the fire. I made him a cup of tea, unheard of except at mealtimes, and sat by him holding his hand to my cheek. He suddenly began to sob. I was afraid. I'd never seen him cry. I put my arms around him .

'Dad, what's wrong?'

'They wouldn't have believed me, lass; they wouldn't.'

Eventually he calmed down enough to tell. The cinema was almost empty but a young girl dressed in high school uniform seated herself beside Dad. After a while she put her hand on his knee. He pushed her hand away but she grabbed his and put it on her thigh. Dad got up and moved to another row but the girl followed him. Again she touched him then whispered that she would scream if he didn't feel her. He panicked, got up and ran. Who would have believed him?

They would have said he was a dirty old man. He never went to the pictures again.

The lad I fancied asked to take me to the pictures. I was cock-a-hoop. A turquoise skirt with its little white circles I had run up myself was ready to wear except for the zip fastener. A good wide belt would hold it up safely, I thought. I was determined to wear this lovely skirt. We met outside and I really enjoyed the film. Just holding hands was as far as any romance went. It was a beautiful night, lovely until I stood up. The skirt fell to my ankles. Quick as a flash I stepped out of it , tucked it under my arm and rushed to the toilet to re-dress. The lad hadn't noticed. I was still embarrassed but put it to the back of my mind.

A few months later I started a new job. The supervisor was introducing me to my colleagues when one loud - mouth piped up, 'Can you remember me telling you about that lass that lost her skirt in the pictures, well this is her.'

As a teenager, I always had two or three boyfriends on the go but was very careful about not getting my dates mixed up.

One week I had a date to meet a boy outside the Savoy at Stanningley at seven-thirty. Then, to my horror, another boyfriend rang work whilst I was in another department and left a message for me to meet him outside the same cinema at the same time, same night. There was no way to contact either of them - few people had telephones at that time - so it looked like I would have to stand them both up, something I rarely did, then hope I could straighten things out later. That same day I met a boy I had been dying to go out with for months and he asked me out too. For safety, I agreed to meet him outside Pudsey Baths at seven. As I got off the bus he saw me, came over and took me back on to the bus.

'I thought we could go to the Savoy,' he said. 'There's a good film on.'

Luckily, when we arrived the other two hadn't. Being a couple, it was usual to sit in the middle at the back. At about seven-forty the other two came in, one down each side, and sat half way down in the cheaper seats. I sweated it out all evening but, miraculously, I never got found out. The boy I'd gone out with turned out to be a big disappointment and we never went out again.

FILM CATEGORIES

Following the setting up of The British Board of Film Censors in 1913, films were originally classified as 'U' (Universal) and 'A' (Adult).

During the early 1930s there appeared a spate of horror films, including some that are now regarded as classics of their genre - *Frankenstein, Dracula, Dr Jekyll and Mr Hyde*, and *The Mummy*. In response to this, in 1933 a 'H' for horror film category was introduced.

The 'X' rating for 'Adult Only' films came into use in 1950.
The first film to receive an X-rating was a French film entitled *Life Begins Tomorrow*. By the end of the sixties the number of X films exceeded the combined total of A and U films released in this country. In 1970 the minimum age for admission to X films was raised from 16 to 18.

The film categories currently in use were introduced in December, 1982 - U for Universal, PG for Parental Guidance, 15 and 18 for the minimum ages for admission, and 18R, a special category for violent or pornographic films which may only be shown in specially licensed cinemas.

இ My first encounter with film categories was in Bradford. I was staying with my aunty in Oak Lane near Lister Mill and the local cinema was showing *Stagecoach* with John Wayne. I was only fourteen at the time. If you went to the early show they would let you in but being a continuous show they banned kids after eight o'clock at night. When I went to pay I blatantly lied that I was just turned sixteen and after some hassle they let me in. I enjoyed the film so much that I decided to see it again but as it started the usherette came round with her torch looking for youngsters. I was right at the end of a row away from the aisle and as her torch shone on me I puffed myself up, trying to make myself look bigger. She wasn't satisfied but I wasn't going to be shown up by giving a lot of hassle so I left quietly.

இ Like most teenage boys, I had a hero. My hero was John Wayne and I think I must have seen every single film that he was in. You know how everyone remembers where they were when John F Kennedy was shot. Well, I know exactly where I was when I heard of John Wayne's death. I was at Filey and I read it on a newpaper billboard. It ruined my day.

„ Once we wagged it off school to go and see *Summer Holiday* with Cliff Richard at the Ritz in Barnsley. Mavis was doing a two year full time secretarial course at the tech and I was doing O levels at the High School. We sneaked out in the dinner hour and changed out of our school clothes in the public lavs in Peel Square, putting on our make-up, tight skirts and stilettos. We stuffed our clobber in our gondola baskets and went to the matinee at the Ritz. It was the first time I had seriously played truant.

„ When I got to courting age the done thing was to take a girl to the pictures. Even better if you could book two seats on the back row in the corner. My first attempt to impress failed miserably. When I looked at the seating plan through the glass window of the booking office I must have got it upside down. I booked what I thought to be the two back seats but when we got there on the night I had booked two seats in the front row. What a fool!

„ On Thursday the girls would pay for the boys to go in because that was when they would be paid. On Friday it was the boys' turn. But by the middle of the week it was, 'I'll meet you inside.' In those days you usually went as a gang or with a couple of lads with the knowledge that - 'If we see anything better inside, then we'll ditch these two.'

„ At fifteen years of age I fell for my husband-to-be in a big way. Over the years to come I would keep seeing him, passing him in the street or youth club.

When I was seventeen I was thrilled because he asked me to go to the cinema with him. But he brought me down to earth when he said, 'Joyce, I'll pay for you in but you'll have to buy your own sweets because I don't eat them.'

After buying a box of *Roses* and placing them on my knee, I went to take one out and found that he had eaten them all bar one!

„ I don't want to make out that we lived in a damp cardboard box but there weren't too many home comforts when I was a lad. It must have been even worse for my mum. She once told me that the first thing Dad had ever bought her was a bar of Toblerone when he took her to the cinema.

Sometimes when I do the family shop I throw a bar of Toblerone into the trolley in memory of my mother.

„ Me and my mate Andy took a couple of girls to the pictures.

'Two one and nines please', said Andy to the woman dispensing tickets.

'I'm not sitting in the one and nines', pouted his escort for the evening.

Without batting an eyelid Andy said 'My mistake. One one and nine love.' And in he went, leaving his date speechless.

„ My friend Winnie and myself arranged to meet two boys to go to our local Bug Hutch. My friend's boyfriend turned up but, alas, mine didn't. Rather than see me disappointed, my friend's partner asked me to go with them. He duly paid for the three of us and I sat at the side of my friend and watched them holding hands, feeling sorry I didn't have a boyfriend to hold mine.

When we came out of the cinema I said my goodbyes. Then he pulled me towards him and said, 'Give me a kiss. You don't think I've paid for you in for nothing, do you?' and he gave me a real smacker whilst my friend looked on.

Feeling embarrassed and flushed I ran home. The outcome was I ended up marrying him and my friend never spoke to me again.

„ I had arranged to meet Geoff at half past seven for our very first date. He was late, very late, and came running up full of apologies just as I was about to get the bus home.

He took me to see *Bloodhounds of Broadway* at The Star and as Mitzi Gaynor sang '*I Wish Someone Like You Could Love Me*' he squeezed my hand. Still cross at being kept waiting, I wasn't talking to him. At the end of the film, as we stood for the Queen, he went deathly pale and fainted.

It was only when he recovered that he told me he'd been knocked off his bike on the way home from work and had been in hospital having five stitches put in his head. That was why he was late. His mother said he was never the same after that night - whether due to me or the knock on the head I'll never know.

It was on the back row of The Star Cinema, where a Tyrone Power film was being shown, that my husband, then my boyfriend, told me he loved me.

When Jane Russell appeared in *The Outlaw* it was supposed to be a very promiscuous film so, of course, everyone just had to see it.

That summer we all wore low-necked, off the shoulder, white blouses and green skirts. I remember my father forbidding me to go to Pontefract dressed like that. He needn't have worried. I must have been invisible as all the girls I met wore them.

Perhaps it was this knowledge that led us all eventually to realise the value of individuality.

I had just got myself comfortably settled on one of those double courting seats when disaster struck. A customer walking in the aisle between the upper and front circle stopped to light a cigarette and carelessly set fire to my hair.

In many ways my weekly visit to the cinema with Mam was a hoot. However, she would insist on buying an ice lolly from the shop before going in and sucking it noisily until it was gone. Was this too high a price to pay for this outing; I ask myself?

There was a film showing at a local cinema, with Rita Hayworth in it. She was very beautiful with long red hair and was a very lively dancer. There was also a romantic story line to the film. I was about fourteen at the time, as were most of my friends.

We all said we were not interested in this film, nevertheless by the following Monday we had all been to see it. At that age we tended to denigrate anything romantic so our comments on the film were not very kind.

A few weeks later, our English teacher asked us to write a story about our dreams. Most of us managed to recount something but I thought it was very funny how many of our dreams contained girls with long red hair with names like Rusty or Sandy. However, the dream girls were usually riding horses or driving cars or swimming - never dancing.

❧The girl in Zefirelli's *Romeo and Juliet* was fifteen years old when I was eighteen. I became obsessed with her and went to the cinema at least four times that week. I can remember on the last night I begged the manager to give me the poster. Although amused by my request, he later did.

Later, I saw it in a small cinema, surrounded by students and became very angry when one of them started laughing during the balcony scene. The fascination continued. Whenever I found it was showing I would travel miles to see it although I was happily married.

Last year it was shown on television and I videoed it. I do not think that I have looked at it from that moment on. I can see it when I wish but now I can think of no reason for wanting to see it. Now that I can have my Juliet whenever I need her, her power has gone. After that the obsession ended. Recently, I looked it up in the Movie Guide. The critic said : 'For all Hussey's prettiness and Whiting's shy charm it is clear that they do not understand one tenth of the meaning of their lines.'

❧ There were only four people in the auditorium when I went to see *Women in Love* - myself, and old woman and a teenage couple. I don't really remember much about the film for no sooner had it started than the couple two rows in front got down to it. Well, at first I tried to ignore it, keeping my eyes on the screen and desperately trying to concentrate on the story. But the grunts and groans were so loud that I began fidgetting and glancing sideways at the old woman. She seemed completely engrossed in the film and oblivious to the happenings two rows in front.

After fifteen minutes of embarrassment I passed onto the disgusted stage, casting filthy glances at the couple, none of which they were aware of. Then, they seemed to suddenly stop and watched the film as if they had been following it from the beginning. The girl even cried at one point.

About twenty minutes before the end they started all over again, only stopping as the credits began to roll. I remember leaving the cinema with not a clue about the story. How desperate they must have been for privacy in order to choose a cinema.

I wonder if the old woman had noticed at all.

PLAY IT AGAIN

Some story lines have particularly caught the imaginations of film-makers. Most popular are, of course, those plots which are 'public property' and do not require payments to authors. Shakespeare, as might be expected, is a common source of inspiration. Over thirty film versions of *Romeo and Juliet* have been made. However, this is not his most popularly filmed play. There have been over sixty different films of *Hamlet*, with leading men ranging from Laurence Olivier to Mel Gibson. In 1987 a Finnish modern-day version was made entitled *Hamlet Liikemaailmassa*. This is set in the world of big business with rival company directors attempting to seize control of the international rubber duck industry.

The story which has been remade the most times is the children's fairy tale, *Cinderella*. There have been nearly one hundred films made based on this famous story. The very first of these, *Cinderella and the Fairy Godmother*, was made as early as August 1898, and starred Laura Bayley as Cinderella. It was probably the first British film to use double exposure and stop action to create 'magic' effects. Since then there have been 'straight', cartoon, ballet versions and even a pornographic version, *The Other Cinderella*, a soft-porn musical made in America in 1976.

The first time I realised that I was not alone was when watching a film at the cinema entitled *Santa Sangre*. A bizarre film - this guy's mother has her arms cut off, I can't remember why. Anyway, the guy decides that he and his mother should become a circus act and he becomes her dancing arms!

I remember noticing things in the darkness and thinking, 'Ooh, they look like a couple - and so do they'. Suddenly it was clear. The entire place was populated by gay men and women. I remember thinking, 'I've come home, Daddy!'

and, as the sun went down, his bum, in profile and slightly out of focus, had gone up and down to noises off-picture.

'Yes,' replied the second woman. They were directly behind us and were on a wives' night out from Garforth.

'I'd expected marriage to be like that but it hasn't been.'

Eventually, if you wanted to see a so-called mucky film then you joined a cinema club but there was a stage in the early 1950s when a number of risque images taken from Italian films, caught the imagination. They really got us

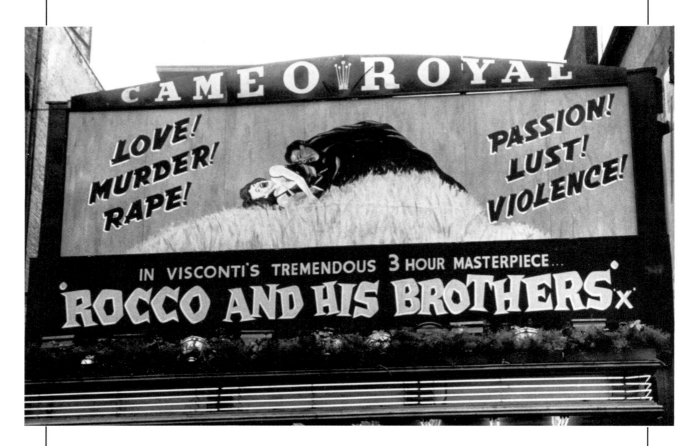

The dialogue in the interval at the Odeon went something like this:

'Wasn't it lovely, the sexy bit'.

The sequence had come in the middle of the first half of *Ryan's Daughter*. The two riders had dismounted by a copse

going but seeing them now they seem tame enough. *Rocco And His Brothers* was one and *Bitter Rice* another. In it the heroine her skirt tucked up into her knicker legs wades through a submerged paddy field. I'd seen more explicit things on the sands at Blackpool but this black and white image has remained with me for forty years.

The *Gone With The Wind* audience was mostly women, with just a smattering of men. The atmosphere was normal enough before the lights went down - chattering and sweet paper rustling. But as time passed the atmosphere got tenser and it was not long before you heard the rustling of kleenex, little sniffles and, eventually, full-throated sobs. In the end one woman rushed up the aisle shouting, 'Oh my God!' .

Longtime Companion was the first major movie about Aids. What you've got to understand is that there is a gay audience which goes to the cinema which is extremely reverential about something serious like Aids, and there is a queer audience which says, 'OK, Aids is here now, let's make fun of it.' A queer audience will look for the black humour; a traditional gay audience won't laugh. You get seriously bitched if you do.

At the Cornerhouse in Manchester when *Longtime Companion* was first shown, we laughed out loud at the hammy acting, the awful lines, the gushing sentimentality of it all. Other gays in the cinema kept shooting us filthy looks but, I mean, if you can't take the mick out of yourselves, who can you take the mick out of?

You went to meet girls, to experiment and, especially, to shout things out.
'I'm coming Cathy, I'm coming,' Heathcliffe cried out.
'That'll be a first'. My mate shouted back.

The film would often break down and people would shout, 'Put another shilling in the slot'.

Just occasionally the projectionist would put a reel on in the wrong order. At the Cape Hill Electric that didn't seem to matter much because as a teenager you went to the cinema for other things - to neck, shout out and make whoppee noises - and not just to watch the film.

Me and my wife went to the cinema only last year. We don't go much and this was a bit of an occasion. We settled down in this very plain but clean auditorium in one of these multi-screen cinemas and set about intending to watch the show. It was all very sedate, all a bit middle-aged - After

Eight mints, that sort of thing.
Half way through, after a bit of flickering, the film broke down and, to my amazement and acute embarrassment, my wife shouted out at the top of her voice, 'Put a penny in the slot!'

We were back in the Shaftsbury again and it was the 1950s.It amazed me that she should react that way. Proof, I guess, that old habits die hard.

I've only ever once heard of a cinema audience clapping a film. We saw *Jigsaw*, a detective film, based on a book by Hilary Waugh. Before the final scenes, when the policeman proved his case, the film stopped and a message came on the screen asking the audience to study all the clues for a few moments. The film then restarted with probably only me knowing the answer - I had read the book. When it finally ended everyone in the cinema applauded spontaneously.

When they showed *Zulu* at the Castle they brought old Mrs Jones from the little shop over in her wheel chair. It was probably the first time she had been in a cinema since the piano and silent movie days but this was something special - this film was about how her brother got his Victoria Cross. The town turned out for the occasion.

Towards the end, when the soldiers are breaking through the partition walls and fighting off the fire, one soldier says to another
'What's your name?'
'I'm Jones from Bwyll Mawr.' To this the other replies,
'I'm Jones from Builth Wells.'
The audience erupted. It's not often you hear Builth mentioned in films.

I suppose that *Educating Rita* was the first film which caused me to think that this might be what it was like seeing life from a woman's point of view. I felt for her being stuck with a bastard like me.

There was a lot to get your teeth into; the husband who was always doing bodged up DIY jobs and then there was that scene where they go to the Working Men's Club and they all start singing. Rita tries to get into the spirit but it is left to her mother to say ,'There must be something better than this.'

❖ I once went to see a sex film in an open air cinema at Bloomington, Indiana, - a place in what has to be described as America's Bible belt. The site was close to the motorway and only separated from it by a high fence. They showed three films a night on an enormous screen. I remember how big everything was and how the surrounding cars started to gently rock during explicit scenes.

❖ I once believed that there should be censorship in the cinemas and I still do where some forms of sexual explicitness are presented. But it's the violence which worries me most. At least in the cinema there is regulation and some control. At the very least there is self-censorship. When it comes to video there is no censorship at all and I worry about what my children might be watching when I am not watching them.

CENSORSHIP

In 1912, fearing that the government would impose censorship on the film industry, the Kinematograph Manufacturers' Association founded their own self-regulatory body, The British Board of Film Censors. This Board was paid for by the industry itself on the basis of a set fee for every foot of film which it viewed.

Two specific rules were laid down for the censors - no nudity and no depictions of Jesus Christ. Its general guidelines were, to quote from its first annual report, the removal of 'anything repulsive and objectionable to the good taste and better feelings of English audiences.'

During its first year, the Board refused to grant a certificate to twenty-two films. The reasons given for cutting films or banning them completely were as follows :

1. Cruelty to animals.
2. Indecorous dancing.
3. Vulgarity and impropriety in conduct and dress.
4. Indelicate sexual situations.
5. Scenes suggestive of immorality.
6. Situations accentuating delicate marital relations.
7. Gruesome murders.
8. Excessively gruesome details in crime or warfare.
9. Indecently morbid death scenes.
10. Scenes tending to disparage public characters and institutions.
11. Medical operations.
12. Executions.
13. Painful scenes in connection with insanity.
14. Cruelty to women.
15. Confinements.
16. Drunken scenes carried to excess.
17. Scenes calculated to act as an incentive to crime.
18. Indecorous sub-titles.
19. Indelicate accessories.
20. Native customs in foreign lands abhorrent to British ideas.
21. Irreverent treatment of sacred or solemn subjects.
22. The materialisation of Christ or the Almighty.

Given this comprehensive list of 'don'ts' it is amazing that of the 7510 films which the Board examined in 1913, only twenty-two were rejected outright.

❧ So, if this is a free country, how come they wouldn't let us see *The War Game*? You could get to see Civil Defence films which told you you would survive if you built a shelter under the kitchen table using doors - if you could get the doors off in less than four minutes that is - and that your chances of survival increased if you placed a paper bag over your head. But you were not allowed to see what the nuclear holocaust, the final four minutes, would really be like.

In the end I saw the film in a pirated edition which someone in the Campaign for Nuclear Disarmament had managed to get from the Quakers. They let it be shown in the Old Town Hall. Hundreds came, I remember. It was so crowded that I ended up sitting on the top of the upright piano.

It was a stark film, with few fancy effects but, because it was cheap and adventurous, it was very, very powerful.

❧ As part of some student teacher's scam to avoid teaching us for an afternoon we visited the film club at York University to see *Culloden*. I went in cold, knowing nothing at all about the English massacre of the Scottish Highlanders and I was stunned. I couldn't watch it at all but I couldn't shut out the sound either so I still knew what was going on.

I disagree with people who think that violence should not be shown on television. I don't watch mindless chain saw massacres and stuff like that, but I do think gore should be shown when it is the outcome of an action you are watching. In my day when the cowboys shot Indians or vice versa it was all glossed over and made OK; well it's not OK so that's why the gore must be shown even though it isn't easy watching.

❧ One film had a big impact on me. I saw it about seventeen years ago. It was called *Soldier Blue*. I saw it in the Cine Centre in Cheapside, Bradford. Everyone had told me about the violence in the film. I thought it wouldn't bother me, but it did. It was just awful and I walked out. My husband thought it was great - he's a typical blood and gore man.

❧ The *Silence of the Lambs* was showing. There were six of us in the cinema, so the lack of people added to the eerie atmosphere of the film. It had just got to the part where Hannibal Lector had ripped off the face of one of his guards when my husband, in a moment of stress, whispered 'I must go for a pee', and disappeared into the depths of darkness. Fifteen seconds later he was back beside me.

'That was quick', I said.

'The toilets are down some stairs and the place is totally pitch black,' he replied. 'There's no way I am going down there.'

He sat there for the rest of the film with his legs crossed, sighing heavily.

❧ When people complain about the disturbing effects of violence in film, why do they never go on to question the value of being disturbed? All good art should unsettle and disturb. Complacency needs to be displaced.

❧ It doesnt matter how often I go to the pictures, I'm always caught by a strange sensation that grips me when I re-emerge into the street. For two hours I've been caught in the killing fields of Cambodia or whatever, only to emerge into the everyday city life of Leeds.

When I watch a matinee film in winter I enter a time warp. It's strange to go into the cinema in broad daylight and come out in darkness. For a couple of minutes I wonder which of the two worlds I'm inhabiting is the most real.

❧ The trip to see *Bambi* was planned as a major occasion. A whole gang went and we occupied almost two rows. The big macho lads were going to have a ball. As it went on, though, I found I couldn't cope. By the time it got to the scene where Bambi's mother dies, my shoulders were heaving and I was sobbing away. I was so embarrassed that I hardly knew what to do but the girl I was with rather liked it. As she said, 'Real men cry.'

❧ Our family legend has it that I offered Bambi my last piece of chocolate!

I must have been very young when my parents had taken me to see Walt Disney's film *Bambi*. I was so wrapped up in the story and was sobbing my heart out for poor Bambi, lost and alone in the forest, that I stood up and through my sobs I said, 'You can have my chocolate, Bambi.'

❧ Compare my six year old daughter's first visit to the cinema and mine. She was in European Disney watching a 360 degree film screen, lasers were bouncing off the ceiling and she was watching actors so big you could see the dirt under Michael Jackson's finger nails.

Aged six, I would be in the stalls of the New Star in Aire Street, afraid that someone would spit on me from the circle and waiting for the red velvet curtains to quietly open to reveal the Pearl Insurance Advertisement. In my hand would be a bag of scraps bought from the chippy next door. In the interval I would go for a pee in the lavatory out back and climb upon the urinal to see Castleford's greatest wonder, the foam forming from the soap powders which rushed over the weir just down from Allison's Mill.

❧ It was the darkness that scared me - being in a darkened room full of strangers. I can understand kids being scared of the wicked stepmother in *Snow White* or of the fire in *Bambi* but I was scared in *Mary Poppins*! It was the blackness. My dad had to carry me out screaming. I never went again until I was in my teens and needed to be somewhere with my first boyfriend.

Stephen McClarence

The film was *The Little Mermaid*. Ian settled himself down next to me. All his friends at nursery had seen the film and talked endlessly about it. As the lights went down he had a big smile on his face and his eyes shone with anticipation. The film started. Ian perched himself on the edge of the seat - riveted. Suddenly the evil sea witch appeared. With one leap he landed petrified in my lap. His arms clasped so tightly round my neck that I could hardly breathe.

'Come on, let's go out if you're so frightened', I said.

' No, no, I want to stay', he said. 'I want to see it, everyone says it's good. Please Mum, don't take me out.'

❧ I took my children and their friends to see *Watership Down*. Most of the kids were enthralled but my youngest son, aged three, was so scared that he cried, quietly, through most of it as I shoved sweets into his mouth.

This son is now sixteen and whenever we hear the song *Bright Eyes* the family still tease him. Recently, I saw the film again. Now I can see why he was so upset; it really is quite frightening. Rabbits getting killed and splattered over the road and black devil rabbits hunting for victims. Now I realise that the film is not really about rabbits at all but society and the down-trodden spending their lives running from authority.

❧ The first film I went to see was *Help*, in 1965, when I was eight. I didn't understand a thing that was going on. I think it was meant to be surreal. It was a relief to discover some years later that it was crap.

❧ One of my earliest memories of the cinema is over sixty years ago when I was about three. For years I have carried a mental picture of me screaming a picture house down and not having the words to tell anyone why.

One Christmas twenty five years later we were all sat round talking about the magic of those days when my mother piped up, 'Do you remember our Harry carrying on demented at The Gaiety when we took him to see *Dante's Inferno*.'

❧ I cannot remember what the main feature was but I have recollections of Mother comforting me because I was upset at the film.

Later, when the Pathe or Movietone Newsreel was showing news of the war, Mother was getting upset so I turned and said, 'Don't worry Mother, it's only a film.'

❧ There weren't many short films going during the war, apart, that is, from pictures of soldiers leaving in troop ships from Southampton. So, as a consequence, we were always getting this film about a blind horse. The first shot would be of a horse eating grass on a hillside. Then you would see his young owner whistle him in. He would gallop down the meadow and run slap bang into a tree.

Blindness has worried me ever since. As a child I wouldn't wander too far, never as far as Normanton Park, just in case I went blind like the horse and couldn't find my way back home.

❧ When I was at the Juniors I learnt about the latest films from my pal, Leonard Wilding. He would keep a small group of us enthralled with a brief synopsis of the film he had seen the previous night. He went most nights because his mom was lonely and picked him up after school.

'What happened then?'

'Well, he was looking for something in the tomb which would keep him alive forever and our man was trying to stop him getting it.'

'What did it look like?' I asked.

'Like tea leaves.' he replied.

The image remains with me. Forty years on I still have the idea that the elixir of life, when found, will look like a soggy mass of tea leaves.

❧ I went to see *The Mummy* when it was first released. It was really good because it left you feeling cold, the way he killed people. I remember when he stamped on one fellows' head. But you had to feel sorry for him, he'd had some rotten luck. He fell in love with a princess. He died for her, then some person brought him back to life. His brother did the dirty on him and pinched his amulet or scarab. Then, once he'd got it back, he only went and drowned himself.

What a film.

❧ My father was a long distance lorry driver and was away quite a lot, so that if my mum wanted to go to the pictures she would meet me from school and take me with her to the teatime performances. As soon as we got settled in the cinema she would bring out the sandwiches and the flask of tea so that we could munch and slurp in the dark.

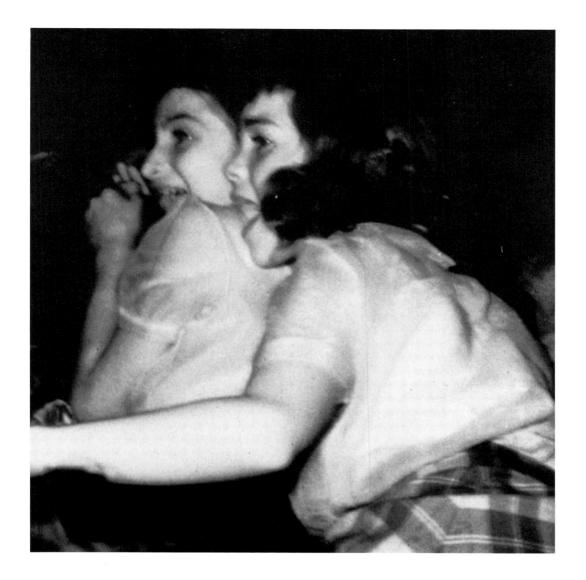

❧ As a small child I went to matinees with my Great Aunt Maggie who would carry with her a large biscuit tin inside a brown paper carrier. She was so tiny she needed this as a footstool. It also held peppermints and liquorice all sorts for during the interval. Mostly we saw Shirley Temple films.

❧ My granny always went to the second house on a Saturday night and, more often than not, I went too. I would go over as soon as I had finished my tea, ready in plenty of time.

If I was spending the night with Granny, which I often did, then all the better. As half past seven arrived she would put on her coat and hand over the bag of sweets which I had been expecting all along. We would walk the two hundred yards to the picture house. Settled in our usual places on the back row of the wooden seats, we waited for the show to start. By this time I had eaten most of the sweets as I had been slipping them into my mouth ever since we left home. I needn't have worried though, my gran would always give me hers as soon as she saw that I wasn't chewing.

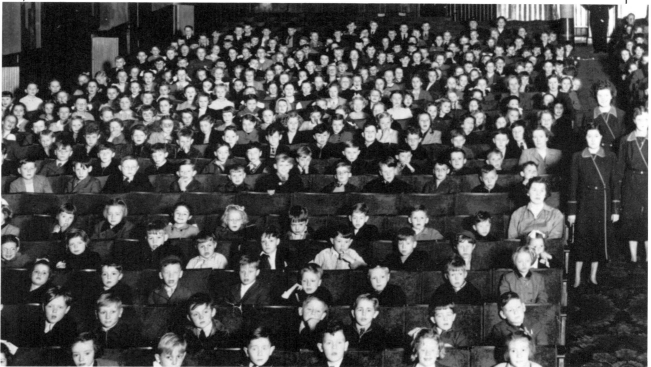

'There he is. Why isn't he at school? If he's poorly why is he at the pictures?'

This went on for some time until I eventually sneaked a look round. It was one of our neighbours with her two kids, both of them in my class at school. I was so embarrassed that I went to the woman on the door and asked if I could go home. She said I could. So, crying, I rushed up the passage to the little window, got my money back and dashed home.

I never saw *Tarzan* and it has never struck me until now that her kids were off school too.

Kids weren't allowed to use the better bookable seats in case we stuck our chewing gum on them. Our favourites were the Three Stooges, Tarzan and, of course, Hopalong Cassidy. In fact, Hopalong appeared at the Hipp so often it was rumoured that he kept his horse in the Feast Ground, and lodged at Southall's sweet shop opposite.

After a cowboy film I would go home, find my mother's lace up pink corsets, make this my saddle and the tailor's buffet became my horse. Then I would ride for miles and conquer the West.

One week I got a bit carried away. This kid had seen these baddies disposing of a body, and they chased him through fields and over hedges, with no houses for miles. The baddies were closing in on him when I started shouting, 'Climb up the tree, hide in the branches.' Guess what? He climbed up the tree and hid in the branches. Well, everyone burst out laughing. One shouted, 'He must have heard her.'

Most films came as twenty-two minute reels but if the projectionist was fed up and it was a cowboy, he would often start it a few minutes into the second reel. All cowboys are basically the same plot so the kids never noticed.

As a child - let's face it, even as an adult - whenever I jump off something high, I shout out loud, 'Geronimo-o-o!' and yet I've never really known why.

My suspicion of its roots is that it must have come from a film. I can see as clearly now, as I have done with every leap, Geronimo jumping out of a first floor window onto the back of a horse, or, alternatively, to his death. On the way down he shouts out his own name. I do realise that my theory doesn't stand up that well to analysis.

The first time I saw a Davy Crockett film I thought, 'That's the hat for me!' Once I got that hat on my scalp, we were destined to become inseparable friends. Neither man nor mother could separate us. Many was the morning when I opened my eyes on the brand new day and cried:

'Mother, where's my hat?' and found it perched like a deceased, over-sized rat on the bedpost.

To create havoc we would load our elastic bands with tin foil and shoot it into the projection beam. If done with others you could produce an effect on the screen which resembled a forest fire.

The *Saturday Stampede*, otherwise known as the *Minor's Matinee* occurred at cinemas all over the country. My haunt was the ABC in Wakefield where, for a few hours and sixpence in old money, kids could escape their parents for a morning or afternoon.

Mr Roberts, the manager, picked one or two quiet customers out and gave them two or three coppers to set the other lads and lasses an example. Then he stood on the stage before the films started with the following oath which we all had to repeat line by line:

We do faithfully promise,
that we will not leave our seats
whatever may happen until the end
of the performance so that all the customers
may both see and hear.

We shouted the last word 'hear' at the tops of our voices.

When the show was over, the row of kids that were the quietest were given a penny each. There were always about half a dozen extra kids in that row that had crawled under the seats to be in at the payout.

If we were among the lucky ones we would put our coppers together and share some broken biscuits and a glass of milk from Castleford market.

I still remember the Gaumont British Saturday matinee song. It summed up the optimism of the years after the war exactly.

We come along on Saturday morning
Greeting everybody with a smile.
We come along on Saturday morning
knowing its well worth while.
As members of the G B Club we all intend to be
good citizens when we grow up
and champions of the free.
We come along on Saturday morning
greeting everybody with a smile, smile, smile
greeting everybody with a smile.

At the Saturday matinee the manager would ask the children if any of them had a birthday that week. If they had, they had to go on the stage and receive a birthday card. This allowed them into the pictures the following week for nothing. Since it was sixpence to go in this meant that you could buy more popcorn and pop than normal. The following week I showed my birthday card I'd received the week before but the usherette never took it from me. This happened on the following two weeks. I felt a cheat but I've never eaten as much popcorn as I did in the weeks following my tenth birthday.

When I was about eight or nine years old the local cinema, The Shaftsbury, started a Saturday morning Cinema Club. When I asked Mum if I could enrol she said, 'Who will fetch the rations?' We've never got on.

You know the memory is a funny thing. While I can't remember what happened last month or last week at times,

I can still remember the *Minors' Anthem* sung at the start of each performance. It went:

We are the boys and girls well known as
minors of the A.B.C.
And every Saturday all line up
To see the films we like
and shout aloud with glee
We like to laugh and have our sing song
just a happy crowd are we
We're all pals together, we're
Minors of the A.B.C.

The serials, they were good. They had us kids sat on the edge of the forms - I can still feel the splinters. My own favourite was The Lone Ranger and his faithful friend Tonto. There was a joke went round that the Lone Ranger had murdered Tonto because he found out what 'Keemo Sabbi' meant.

The Tom Thumb Club in Featherstone was sponsored by a local newspaper. I was never a member but I always went to the Saturday pictures. The cinema was full of kids, a noisy affair, and the usherettes had a job to keep them quiet. Eventually, if the noise got too bad, Bob Jackson, the owner would put on the lights and bang a biscuit tin to get order. He didn't mind the cheering or booing but objected to us getting restless during the kissing scenes.

The first time I went to the cinema I went with my older sister. I'd be six or seven and she would be eight, so when I learnt that the only way to go to the lavatory was to go next door to Hannah Law's parents I had no option but to pee myself. I remember standing there and watching the rivulet making its way across the dusty floor towards the front of the picture house. My sister was so ashamed.

If I wanted to go to the cinema mid-week and my parents didn't want to go or couldn't afford to go, I would go on my own. Often the film classification meant a child could not get in unless accompanied by an adult, so I would stand outside and ask any couple if they would take me in. The secret was to find a couple who were going in the same price seats as I would only have money for the cheap seats.

<blockquote>If it was an 'A' film you had to be with an adult. I can remember this old man who used to take all the kids in. All the kids used to go to him. I think he was called Jimmy and he would get the tickets and once inside the cinema all the kids used to go their own way. He always had a bag of mint imperials. My mother was a bit concerned when I talked about him and, to my surprise, decided to go with me to the cinema one evening. That was very unusual. I now know it was because she wanted to check out who this Jimmy was.</blockquote>

<blockquote>I slept with a Hollywood actress when I was seven years old. She was about two inches tall, made of card and came out of a sweet cigarettes packet. She was the actress who played Helen of Troy in a fifties film version I saw in the Rock Cinema in my home village of Cudworth.

The moment she appeared on the screen I fell truly, madly, deeply in love with her.

A few days after seeing this film I bought a packet of sweet cigarettes and when I opened them to my great delight there she was again, tucked in behind the fags.

I took her upstairs to my bedroom. Helen of Troy in bed with me! Wow! Wait until I tell my mates!</blockquote>

❧ I was a lad in the mid-fifties - the golden age of cinema. As a lonely fifteen year old, I always used to search out obscure flea pits where a film I was interested in was showing. I usually emerged, head spinning, around nine in the evening, or as late as my last bus home would permit. Not something a child could do on their own these days, even if the cinemas still existed.

Even today, on the rare occasion I go to the cinema, I still feel short measured when usherettes hang around for you to leave after just one showing.

❧ I was at Bolton School around about 1955 and establishing an astronomical society. I decided to put on a big film show for the members and managed to hire a black and white 16mm print of the film *Destination Moon*.

Besides plastering the school with posters advertising the show, there was much kudos in having the headmaster announce the forthcoming event during morning assembly. We managed to attract an audience of around a hundred, at a shilling a time, to defray the hire costs - quite an achievement

This was my first venture into show business. In later life I went on to run my own Planetarium at Scarborough.

❧ My mother took my young sister and me for a teatime showing of *Grease*. We watched gob-smacked throughout, transfixed by adolescent Travolta-infatuation and wishing we could live the all-American life of high school gossip and tight leather trousers. How I wished I was Olivia Newton John, with pierced ears and an exciting gang of girlfriends.

So obsessed were we, that we hid in the toilets at the end of the film and sat equally transfixed through the evening showing. The mania continued when we persuaded our parents to buy the Pickwick cheap version of the sound track and other hits from the film: *You're The One That I Want*, *Summer Nights* and *Hopelessly Devoted To You*.

I'm not sure when my own Travolta infatuation died, it was probably when I swapped my *Grease* pillowcase for an equally tacky pencil box.

❧ A film I saw as a teenager shaped my political consciousness. At the end of the great epic when the revolt of the Roman slaves has been suppressed Laurence Olivier asks the assembled prisoners, 'Who is Spartacus?' Kirk Douglas comes forward. He says, 'I'm Spartacus.' As he stands there awaiting punishment Tony Curtis steps forward and also proclaims, 'I'm Spartacus.' Then, one after another, every prisoner steps out: 'I'm Spartacus' - 'I'm Spartacus' - 'I'm Spartacus.' That film made me a Communist.

They reckon that at Orgreave, during the miners' strike in 1984, the colliers re-enacted something like that in front of the police, so don't tell me that films cannot radically affect peoples lives. We are not just influenced by reason. Poetry and metaphor also shape us.

❧ It was about eleven-thirty when we left the pub and headed for the late night showing of *Friday The 13th* at the local picture house. It was raining outside so no-one thought it strange that we all wore long coats in the middle of June.

There were about fifteen of us that night as we entered the cinema and headed upstairs to the front row of the balcony. As usual, in this cinema on a Friday night, the air was thick with the smell of booze and dope. People were laughing and joking as they waited for the film to start. Then, with a drunken cheer, the lights dimmed, the curtains drew back and the previews began.

That's when we put our plan into action. Under cover of darkness we all took off our coats, under which each of us had part of a Guy Fawkes-type dummy. All the parts were passed along the row and carefully fitted together. Finally we put on it a rubber mask, brown curly wig and one of the raincoats we had arrived in earlier Our creation assembled, we sat back and enjoyed the film.

When the film had ended and everyone had been frightened by Jason jumping out of the water, my friend stood up and shouted, 'I can't take any more!' and we launched the dummy from the balcony. Chaos erupted from the seats below. After we had finally stopped laughing we decided it would be best to leave, but our way down from the balcony was blocked by the manager who asked us to stay seated until the police arrived. It turned out he had phoned the police and an ambulance before finding out it

was a dummy. The ambulance had been cancelled, but the police had not.

They arrived about fifteen minutes later, by which time we had all moved away from the balcony and mingled with other people up there.

The police, with their usual quest for amusement, refused to see the funny side and threatened to arrest everybody if the culprit did not own up.

After about thirty minutes of banal questions and thoroughly bored of the whole thing, my friend slowly rose to his feet and declared, 'I am Spartacus.' I quickly followed by standing and shouting, 'No, I am Spartacus,' swiftly followed by everyone else all shouting, 'I'm Spartacus, no, I'm Spartacus!'

It was 1953 and the local cinema was showing the newly-released George Pal film of H G Wells' *War Of The Worlds*. Being a space nut then - and still now - I was determined to get in to see what I knew would be a classic. Trouble was the hierarchy at the British Board of Film Censors had declared it to be an X film, which meant that no-one under the age sixteen years could be admitted.

Undeterred by my fifteen years I sneaked in and have never regretted it.

That film was shown on television a couple of years ago - in the Saturday Matinee children's slot - so much for censorship! How times change.

I was only twelve when I went to see Mr Gill at the Majestic, Howden, and asked him if I could be the assistant projectionist.

He said, 'Yes,' but added that he thought I ought to call round to see Sergeant Rex to get his approval.

'Well me lad,' he said, 'If you want to do it I don't see why not. The only thing is tell Mr Gill that he'll have to blindfold you if it's an X film.'

I remember the first X certificate film that I managed to get into the cinema to see.

The film showing was one of the first Hammer Horror Films, *The Curse of Frankenstein*. Well I knew it was going to be a bit more realistic than the old Boris Karloff films with a great white-faced sort of lumbering figure with a flat head, big boots and bolts sticking out of his neck but for me it turned out to be a bit too realistic. I managed with the help of a bag of Butterkist pop corn, a tub of Walls ice cream and a drink on a stick to sit through the first part. This showed gory details of building the monster and consisted of digging up a corpse and then adding bits pinched from out of the morgue.

By this time I was shaking and when I closed my eyes and tried to pretend I was somewhere else I could still imagine what was going on and it was worse. Then, as the music grew more menacing, I opened my eyes and saw the thing climb out of it's tank and grab hold of Frankenstein by the scruff of the neck and start strangling him. That was the end for me. I was off up the aisle running. I had the idea that strangling was in vogue at that moment and I was next in line.

We didn't go to the pictures much, just up to the Scrat in Airedale to see films like *Zorro* or *Flash Gordon And The Clay People* , so it was a bit of a treat to go from school to see a real film like *Henry V*.

What was most memorable was how they changed from the little Elizabethan theatre to the realistic battlefields and back to painted sets. It was as if they were leaving the stage behind and getting into something much bigger. I'd never read it then and I've not read it since but I've some clear memories. There is the bit where the King shouts 'God for England. Hurray for St George,' and the armoured French horses get ready to charge.

Thinking back I don't remember much about what was said though I think that it must have been easier to understand if you were a northern council house kid than if you were a youth from a leafy southern suburb. We said *thee* and *thou* naturally so, in that sense, Shakespeare's speech wasn't so different from our playground talk.

The first film I ever saw was *The Song of Bernadette*. I was at a convent school and this was considered suitable. The film was about St Bernadette of Lourdes, the young girl who had visions of the Virgin Mary. Some parts affected me badly as it showed victims of bubonic plague and I had nightmares about it for ages. The strangest thing though was that I convinced myself that I had seen a vision of Mary.

Films affect me. I don't usually take much interest in politics or world affairs but after I had seen *Cry Freedom* , the story of Steve Biko's death in South Africa, I said to myself, 'What gives them the right to do that to anyone?'

To me, such films have much more power than real events. That's because a film can take you into the story and let you see what made the situation, whereas something on television gets there by chance; the television crew was there because they weren't somewhere else.

A number of people my age remember the filmed pictures of the opening up of Belsen concentration camp. This surprises me because usually film managers insisted that children were removed from the auditorium at the point where this part of the newsreel was shown. Yet two of us, both nine at the time, remember the same sequence, a bulldozer pushing corpses into a mass grave, so we must have slipped through the net.

I have conflicting attitudes as to whether I should have seen that type of horror at such an early age. Some things ought not to be shown to young children but, on balance, I am glad I saw this. My father was quite anti-Semitic. I learnt from the newsreel where any form of race hatred gets you.

In Germany in the 1960s they knew that film would influence you and, therefore, every secondary school child had to go to see one about the holocaust. I was about eleven but I still remember the mountains of shoes, the room packed with hair and, to this day, I cannot see a particular type of shower head without thinking of Auschwitz.

As a boy I queued with my parents to see *Jaws* at the Picture House in Castleford, an event I clearly remember, although not quite as clearly as my father. He tells a story of how we were standing behind a group of Germans and as a point of information he said to me, 'Those people in front of us are Germans.' I, apparently, was puzzled. The only Germans I had ever seen wore grey uniforms, funny shaped hats and were often rounded up by the good guys. I turned to my father and said, 'If they're Germans, Dad, then where are their guns?'

Who did we working class kids boo and who did we cheer? We always booed Hitler, Mussolini and Tojo and cheered Stalin, President Truman and Generalissimo Chiang Kai-Shek. Churchill was an odd case. We cheered him up to the end of the war, when we saw him greeting the Eighth Army in North Africa and giving people the victory sign, or touring the bombed cities in his siren suit. But after his defeat at the polls and the Labour victory we booed and booed and booed.

A regular customer, three times a week, was Jack Hodgkiss, the stammering grocer. Whenever there was an unusual twist in the plot or when the villain was exposed, Jack could be heard exclaiming, 'Well, I'll be buggered!'

SUNDAY OPENING

The Cinematograph Act of 1909 was primarily concerned with regulating fire and safety procedures in cinemas. It also had the effect, however, of giving local authorities the power to impose other conditions relating to cinema operations in their area. The strength of the religious moralists' lobby, well represented on town councils, was such that in many towns, cinemas were forced to close on Sundays.

The situation was confused by the fact that although some cinemas were open on Sundays, all theatres were closed. Theatres came under the legislation of the Sunday Observance Act of 1780 which forbade live stage shows on the Sabbath.

In 1931 the Sunday Observance Act was interpreted to also cover film performances and all cinemas were forced to close their doors on Sundays. Such was the public outcry over this decision, however, that in 1932 a Sunday Entertainments Act was passed. This Act put the decision whether or not to allow Sunday film-going back in the hands of the local authorities. Consequently, Sunday opening varied greatly, depending on which part of the country you happened to live in. In London, nearly all cinemas were open seven days a week whilst in the 'Bible belt' of rural Wales, you were as likely to be able to buy a pint of beer on a Sunday as watch a film in your local cinema.

It wasn't until the war that our local cinema opened on a Sunday. We had a lot of Polish troops stationed near us and I suppose they thought that it would be good for morale if they could go to the pictures on Sunday evening. It was also good if any of our lads were home on leave. They only got a few days and wanted to make the most of their time at home, so Sunday opening was essential. Some people kicked up a fuss at first but the protests soon died down. We had more important things to worry about.

There was a big conflict of interest in our house. Mum was Baptist and very much against the pictures, whereas Dad was a sign writer who made a few bob on the side doing posters for the local cinema. When the magistrates in our town relaxed the rules on Sunday showings he was in a position to earn some extra money. The Cape Hill Electric could only compete with the Odeon if it changed its programme on the Sabbath. He now had to do three, rather than two, posters each week and we had jam on our bread. Mum tut-tutted but didn't try too hard to stop him.

The Lord's Day Observance Society was the real force which opposed Sunday opening and a big man in the LDOS was called Martin. The Daily Mirror referred to him as 'Misery Martin'. He was in the vanguard of the opposition to Sunday cinema opening. Once, to prove that he didn't even have to use public transport on a Sunday, he walked all the way from London to Brighton.

I often used to take my teenage sister to the pictures but dreaded taking her into the auditorium if the film had already started. She would stand in the aisle for ages, transfixed by the screen and not bothering to look for a seat.

One particular time, I lost my patience. I grabbed her around the waist and pushed her along a row of disgruntled people to two empty seats. It was not until I had her firmly seated that the usherette's torch shone in her face. Then I realised that my sister was already seated, enjoying the film, two rows behind.

I'd never seen my dad cry. 'Oh George, you're crying,' my mam said. 'Don't be so bloody daft', he replied. But I'd already seen him wipe his eyes when he thought that I wasn't looking.

It happened when we went to see *The Long Grey Line*, starring Tyrone Power and Maureen O'Hara. It's a film I've never seen on television. It was about him being in the army. I don't remember too much about the story though I do know that he called his men 'my buckos'.

Wilf, my husband, has seen it more recently. He said it was a load of rubbish.

'Don't sit down there, we shall be too near me dad and we know what he is like,' said Fran, so we headed towards the back downstairs.

The first film we saw was a short cowboy with the train coming blaring down the track straight at the audience. Someone at the front shouted, 'Duck!' and the first three rows duly obliged. The picture house erupted with laughter.

'Me dad again,' said Fran. 'There's one thing, we do see life at the pictures.'

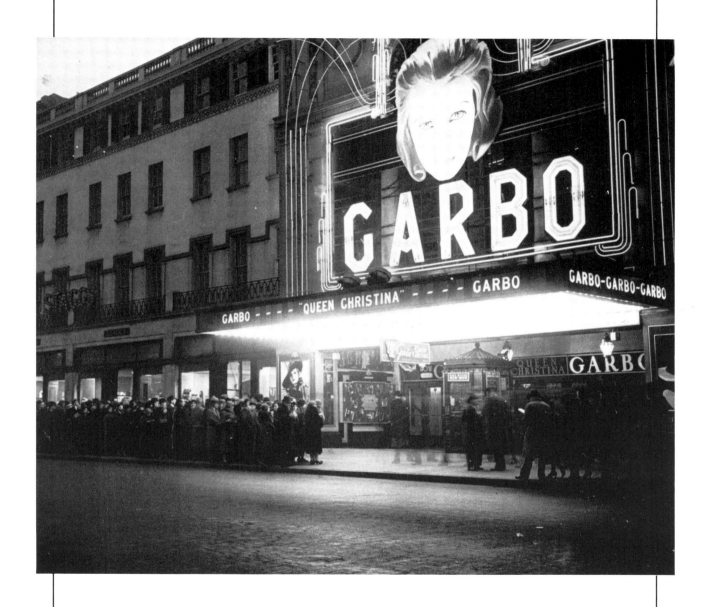

*I feel that our local flea pit deserves
a place amongst the listed buildings of the world.
It still stands today but it is now a bingo hall.*

CHAPTER THREE

THEY WERE LOUSY PICTURE HOUSES BUT WE SAW SOME GREAT FILMS

❧ It is part of family history that Uncle Owen Brookes who lived in a scullery house, 4 Wilton Place, Leeds was a close friend of Louis Le Prince, the first man to produce a moving image - a sequence of images showing traffic moving across Leeds Bridge.

The story is well known. Le Prince had got the collated notes of three men - Uncle Owen was one of them - when he boarded a train in France and disappeared off the face of the earth. There was a sinister plot and within a few months the American, Edison, had come up with moving pictures. A lot believe that Edison had him knocked off.

Uncle Owen went on though with his experiments, once even being arrested as an anarchist because he would hide beneath a cloth when taking pictures. This, of course, was a strange thing to happen to a staunch Methodist.

❧ One of my mother's treasured possessions is a portrait of Anna Neagle, signed by her some time in 1942. She has written across her collar 'With admiration for your great work in the early days of the film world.'

She sent the photograph because my grandfather, Bertram Bernard of Phil and Bernard, had been responsible for making one of the first ever hand-coloured films. It showed the Diamond Jubilee of Queen Victoria, as the procession passed to St Paul's. In 1897 a thousand feet of that particular sequence was shown at the Alhambra, Leicester Square, following three painstaking months of frame by frame colouring.

I assume that Anna Neagle was interested in this slice of film history because she was the star of *Sixty Glorious Years*.

❧ Grandfather spent part of his life taking his kinematographic displays all over the country. In 1897 he was showing *A Full Cavalry Charge*, *On A Belgian Beach* and other shorts to audiences up and down the country as part of a package of live shows and films. The novelty value was attractive. In November 1900 his Rayograph productions would bring him £8.00 for six nights.

He later got invoved in cinema management and by the time he retired he was showing talkies. Once started, technical developments came very quickly.

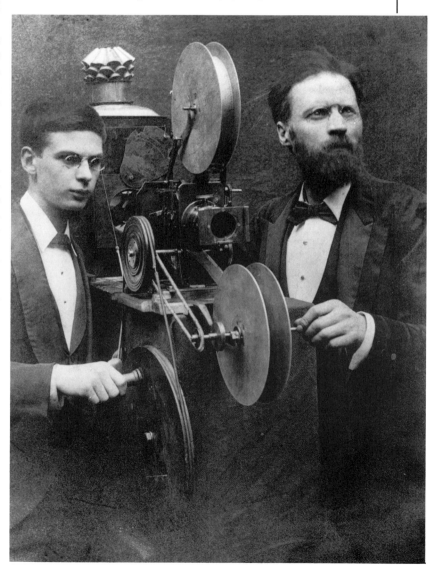

They say that Jasper Redfern, who also had an optician's shop, started to make and show films in Sheffield in 1896 - that's very early on for film-making - but he definitely did put on picture shows with variety turns down in the Central Hall, Norfolk Street, between 1905 and 1912. They were rather crude, all flicker. What fascinated us was the movement. Moving was the thrill. You sat on wooden forms and the complete show lasted no more than twenty minutes.

One, I remember, was of Houdini the escapologist. It showed him arriving at Midland Railway Station. I went as a boy and got a stick of rock. Mr Redfern could see the benefits of selling things, though I think the rock was free, and, therefore, he employed women with baskets of oranges to sit outside. Things don't change much. When I retired we were still making good money from ice creams and drinks on sticks.

THE FIRST CINEMAS

At first, films were shown in any convenient premises that were suitable for a seated audience. Theatres, music halls, lecture halls and similar buildings were hired by the early showmen.

It was not until the early years of this century that the first purpose-built cinemas appeared. The first purpose-built cinema in Britain was the Central Hall, Colne in Lancashire, opened in 1907. It is still standing but ceased to operate as a cinema in 1924.

These early cinemas closely followed the design and interior decoration of the contemporary music hall and were built complete with a proscenium arch, stage, orchestra pit and a circle. Even ticket pricing was based on theatre practices - it was common to charge more for seats at the front of the stalls than at the back.

My grandmother was an entertainer. She presumably met my grandfather when he was taking his cinematograph shows round the music halls. From what I am told he was doing this at the end of Queen Victoria's reign. If this is true, then we must be one of the oldest families anywhere who can trace their history back to the very earliest days in cinema.

We opened the Wicker Cinema with Lillian Gish in *Broken Blossoms* and filled the hall from top to bottom with flowers. Remember, this was a working class area on the edge of town with factories and back-to-back houses coming quite close to us. Many of the people who came weren't expecting to find this sort of glamour.

Our girls dressed as Chinese maidens and in the interval one of them walked up and down the centre aisle swinging what looked to be an expensive incense burner but was really an old glue pot heated with glowing charcoal.

We loved to keep the Wicker fresh and so we sprayed perfume after each show. A lot of attention went into that aspect of the work.

During the Irish Rebellions which took place just after the First War the Sherwood Foresters were stationed in Queenstown, I think. The battalion entertainments manager took over the projector which we had confiscated when we were part of the Army of the Rhine and set it up in the dining hall. He charged sixpence to come in and must have made a fortune.

It wasn't the ideal place. The soldiers used to wipe their knives and forks on the screen as they came out.

There was one part of the auditorium to avoid at the Grand West Bar and that was the area below the circle side aisle. Patrons used to come and tiddle over the balcony. The seats there were always a bit damp.

The Regent, Sheffield, opened on Boxing Day 1927. When I was ten I chose to go as a Christmas treat rather than visit the pantomime. I had little interest in the film- Mary Pickford in *My Best Girl* - I had come to see the cinema organ. Three years before, I had seen Blackpool's organ, heard a rendition of *The Storm* and became fascinated.

Although we queued right round the building I was not disappointed. This was a real picture palace.

The stairs swept splendidly upwards and the auditorium was dominated by a magnificent dome. The carpets were so thick that I could have done the breast stroke through them. My dad was a tram driver. I wasn't used to seeing this sort of luxury.

At the interval a page boy dressed in a red uniform came onto the stage with an easel on which he placed a card saying the Leslie James would entertain us. This was quickly followed by the organ rising out of the orchestra pit with the

53

Where I grew up in Hunslet there were a lot of picture houses all within a few minutes walk away. The best one was the Strand on Jack Lane but there was also the Regal on Low Road and the Picturedrome on Waterloo Road. The one we went to on Saturday was the Premier on Saynor Lane. The seats - I use the term loosely - were a few rows of wooden forms. Girls sat on one side, boys on the other. Woe betide anyone who sneaked on the other side. They had proper seats but they cost more. They were 7d, 9d and 1/3d.

There were at least six large cinemas within spitting distance of Rodley where we lived. If we caught a bus in any direction - there were plenty of those too - we must have had hundreds of cinemas to choose from.

Going to the cinema was part of eveyone's life in those days, though I never understood for a long time what my uncle meant when he used to answer our questions of where had he been, by giving the same retort, 'I've been to t'Colli t' see Tom Mix.'

I knew that 't'Colli' was the Colliseum in Cookridge Street in Leeds, but who was Tom Mix?

My schoolfriend lived in the country and her cinema had a corrugated tin roof. When it rained the noise was deafening and you couldn't hear the film. Local lads added to the chaos by whistling and jeering and the manager often stopped the film until they settled down. There was only one gramophone record which was played before the programme started and again at the end: the Ink Spots singing *Whispering*.

We went to the little cinema in Oakenshaw, somewhere at the back of Wike to see Bill Haley And His Comets in *Rock Around The Clock*. Two steps up and you were in the balcony for 2d, two steps down and you were in the stalls. Well, we had heard that people were ripping out the seats to dance. We didn't do that but we jived in the aisles and in front of the screen.

That went on until, in a cloud of dust, the floor gave way.

I saw *Rock Around The Clock* at the long-demolished Saltaire Gaumont. The performance I attended was full to capacity with a fair sprinkling of Teddy Boys in the audience. A row of policemen were standing along the wall at the back of the stalls.

The patrons were clearly present for the music only and made this apparent by a collective groan whenever the film cut away from it to concentrate on some fatuous piece of dialogue. Occasionally one of the bolder Teddy Boys would entertain the rest of us with a spot of jiving in the aisle while the floor beneath us reverberated to the massed tapping of feet.

The atmosphere was entirely good-humoured and, as far as I could tell, the policemen were not called upon to arrest anyone. Since they were all young, perhaps they were too absorbed in the music themselves.

We had the Majestic, The Rink, The Empire, The Grove, The Beacon, The Electric, The Windsor; grandiose names for picture houses in a dull little town but it was in these picture palaces that I got a feel for a world miles away from our house and our street.

I saw Jimmy and Tommy Dorsey in the *Dorsey Story*, I saw Brando in *A Street Car Named Desire,* Mario Lanza in *The Great Caruso* and Mel Ferrer walking around on his knees pretending to be Toulouse Lautrec in *Moulin Rouge*. My interest in jazz, theatre, opera and fine art didn't spring from good teaching but from picture houses.

My childhood was the golden age of the cinema. I went to see classics when they first came round the pictures which my thirty-year-old film buff son raves about.

Remember, everyone smoked in those days and half-way through the big film there was always something like a dense fog hanging in the roof of the cinema and slowly descending into the beam. The manager's advice was straight forward enough.

'If the buggers are soft enough to smoke then they'll have to freeze. Put the fan on for the last half hour.'

You'd hear them say as they came out, 'Bye, it were chilly at the end.'

CINEMA NAMES

How many cinema-goers ever pause to consider the origins of the names of their favourite flea pits? Some of the most popular names can be traced back as far as the Golden Age of ancient Greece.

LYCEUM. The lyceum was the garden in Athens in which Aristotle taught philosophy. By extension the name came to signify any place associated with education or teaching took place, such as a lecture hall. Eventually it was used for any place where groups of people met - theatres, music halls and, of course, cinemas.

HIPPODROME. The name Hippodrome is derived from two Greek words, 'hippos', meaning horse, and 'dromos', meaning race. As the combination suggests, it originally referred to a place where horse or chariot races were held. It gradually came to be used to describe a place where popular entertainment was staged - hence the name for a cinema.

Other names have a more recent and prosaic origin.

RITZ. Ritz was a Swiss hotel owner who lived during the last century. He founded a chain of hotels that were famous for the degree of luxury which they provided. The adjective 'Ritzy' soon came into popular use to describe anything which was conspicuously luxurious. In the minds of the audience, any cinema called the Ritz must, by association, provide them with above average comfort and service.

One Boxing Day at the beginning of the war I had a half crown. I went to the Picture House in Castleford to the afternoon matinee. After the show, I went to the New Star with a quarter of chocolates for the first house show. Later I went straight to the Theatre Royal second house and bought a tub of ice cream during the interval. That's the only certain treble I've ever done.

I feel that Featherstone's only cinema, The Hippodrome, deserves a place amongst the listed buildings of the world. It still stands today, like many other picture houses, as a bingo hall.

The Empire Cinema was a single storey building, therefore the best seats were at the back. The first eight rows cost one shilling. I didn't need my torch to tell me where the shilling rows began because that was where the carpet stopped. From this dividing line there was no carpet between the seats, just wooden floorboards.

The next few rows cost nine pence. At the last row of the ninepenny seats there was a silk rope across the aisle, this was to separate the best end of the cinema from the 'Chicken Run,' where the seats cost just sixpence. The people in the sixpenny seats had to come into the cinema by a different door. The rope segregated them from their more affluent neighbours.

Sometimes the cinema would intersperse the two major films with a stage presentation. I recall even now attending the Gaumont, Streatham, when, at different times, I saw the singer Hutch, the Two Leslies and mock-Egyptian sand dancers, Wilson, Kepel and Betty.

Every week we had a guest, who came from the world of music or acting, call in at the matinee. I think the first inkling that all might not be what it seemed came with the guest appearance of Dicky Valentine. I was twelve and I had swooned over his romantic songs and dreamed of his lips. What we got was this short, rather podgy, ordinary older man. That's when I had all my lusting thrown back at me.

≈During the war my grandmother lived close to a United States Air Force base in Scotland. Her and a friend went to see a Burt Lancaster film and throughout there was a lot of commotion from some of the airmen seated a couple of rows behind them.

Gran and her friend kept shushing them and for a couple of minutes at a time they had some success. When the lights went up at the interval, Gran turned round to give them a piece of her mind and got a huge shock. Suddenly the reason for all the noise became clear. Burt Lancaster sat there smiling good-naturedly as his friends took the mickey out of his performance.

≈ I've few pictures of myself when I was a teenager but there is a newspaper picture of me queing to be an extra in *Blue Scar*. Although I shouldn't say so, I look like a real glamour girl.

≈ Working at the Wimbledon tennis championships you see a lot of famous faces. The canteen and staff bars are full of gossip about which star did this and which royal did that. Before long you start feeling left out unless you have some cool anecdote about a star, the bigger the better.

I saw my fair share of film stars but they were mainly walking between courts or sat watching the tennis, no real anecdotes to impress the waitresses with, although Tatum O'Neal was a real picture. The best story I heard about a film star over my three years at the tennis was one from a barman who served Clint Eastwood. Clint approached the bar and asked for a bottle of beer, the barman replied in his best Wimbledon voice, hungry for a tip, 'Would you like a glass with that sir?' To this Clint replied 'Heroes don't drink out of glasses.'

I was in Hong Kong at the same time as the film *The Ferry To Hong Kong* was being made. I was in the navy and we were in port to refit our ship, HMS Crane. The film crew wanted some extras for a scene in the film where a lot of men walk off the ferry in smart suits. They approached our ship for some men and the First Lieutenant promptly lined us all up and picked the lucky ones out. There I stood in a bright suit with a rolled collar and half moon pockets. I didn't stand a chance. William Holden was the star of the film and we used to watch him go by on the ferry all the time. We used to wave at them shouting 'All them who are puffs, wave.' Of course Holden and the rest waved back.

I got the job of being an extra when Twentieth Century Fox were filming *Journey To The Centre Of The Earth* at Edinburgh University in 1959 I stepped in complete with kilt. So when you see the professor, played by James Mason, being cheered off on his voyage by the students in the University quadrangle, watch out for me - I am at the left on the back row. It's available from all good video stores.

On my travels I met up with all sorts of people on the way I'd spend a few days travelling with them then we'd head off in different directions. One guy I met up with had just come out of Thailand where he'd been making a bit of money as an extra in the film *Platoon*. He dug into his bag and pulled out an amazing photograph of himself in full costume with his face all greened up. It was an impressive photo, he looked totally realistic. He then told me that he'd sent copies off to his family and friends back home with the simple message

'Joined up. Can't say much. See you in six months.'

'Go on sucker, make my day!' A cinema cliché that has entered into popular language. But where were you when you first saw Dirty Harry point his magnum at the temple of some Californian thug? I know exactly where I was. I was in New Hall Detention Centre for bad lads near Wakefield, doing three months for selling cannabis to my mates. A massed congregation of car thieves, muggers, burglars and gang leaders sat in a hushed dining room to watch Clint Eastwood mete out summary justice on thieves, muggers

and gang leaders. The screws squeaked up and down the polished floor in their ill-fitting boots, flicking back their hair and talking like they'd got cigars in the corner of their mouths. A lad sitting next to me who had got six months for hitting his next door neighbour with a chain, got more and more excited with every shooting, until I was sure his knuckles would pop.

Later on, as I took my weekly shower with the rest of the great unwashed, I'm sure I heard one seventeen year old Dirty Harry say, 'Go on sucker, make my day!'

Per Ardua Ad Astra - Through effort to the stars; the proud motto of the Royal Air Force. But to National Service men it meant: 'Forget bull night; let's go to the pictures. That's because all cinemas on all RAF stations were called The Astra. Ours was a tiny hundred-seater on the station I served at in Berlin.

On this particular evening in 1959 we had done our bull and sought refuge in the Astra. The film showing on the almost twenty foot wide cinemascope screen was *The Big Country*, starring Gregory Peck.

It was a tiny cinema, and all ranks rubbed shoulders; from the Commanding Officer and his lady to the lowliest erk and his woman. The film was under way, a towering, spectacle with stirring stereophonic music, in glorious, technicolour and, of course, Cinemascope. The tiny screen was standing up to the strain remarkably well.

It was also a very long film with a break in the middle to allow us to replenish our stocks of sweets, crisps and popcorn. Something to rattle during the performance was compulsory.

In front of us Jim sat enthralled and munching both crisps and popcorn. It was nearing the halfway point; the music rose to a crescendo, the word 'Intermission' appeared, spilling off both ends of the screen, the lights went up and we all filed out for re-fills.

On returning to the auditorium for the second half we noticed that Jim had retired. Later we found him in the Corporals Club.

'You didn't think much to the film then, Jim?'

'Damn silly ending, if you ask me,' he replied.

Literacy is a wonderful thing.

All the big cities had a News Theatre. The Sheffield one was in the square where Edward's statue stands. The Birmingham one close to Dale End. When I think of it, both were at bus terminuses. That was probably deliberate because the shows seemed to last exactly an hour - a short length of time, the sort of period you might use up between the end of shopping and going home.

Each programme consisted of a couple of news programmes, one which began with a cockerel crowing and another which had wireless waves coming from a mast. Then there was an instruction film of some sort. It might be about anything; how factory farming would produce better eggs or what the tower block cities of the future would be like. Then there would be a cowboy short or a cartoon. *Looney Tunes* was popular. Travelogues were popular and they did really end with lines like 'And as the sun sinks slowly in the west we bid farewell to this....'

NEWSREELS

Some of the first films ever made were of 'News' events. In June 1895, the film pioneer Birt Acres recorded the opening of the Kiel canal by Kaiser Wilhelm 11. The celebrations for Queen Victoria's Silver Jubilee in 1897 were the subject of a number of films.

The first newsreel to be made in Britain was produced in 1906 and entitled *Day To Day*.

The two most famous newreels in this country were Movietone News and Pathe News. Movietone News was founded as British Movietone in 1929 and was the first British newsreel to use sound. The first issue, on 9 June 1929, covered the Derby and the Trooping of the Colour. The very last issue of Movietone News was released almost exactly fifty years later, on 27 May 1979. By this time, largely because of television news coverage, its popularity had declined to one tenth of its peak during the Second World War.

I joined the WRAC when I was seventeen and, after basic training in Guildford and Yeovil, was posted to Belgium attached to an RAOC depot. It was only a little unit, in the backwoods outside Antwerp and there was, of course, no cinema on camp. However, one of the lads in HQ Coy had been on an AKC (Army Kinema Corps - the K distinguishing it from the ACC which is the Army Catering Corps) course for projectionists. After that he hired a projector and films off the AKC and showed films in the cookhouse dining room. We sat on canvas, sling-bottom stacking chairs which very quickly led to numb-bum syndrome, and so on film nights we would head for the cookhouse with our pillows under our arm. We had some good films. In particular I

remember seeing *Lawrence Of Arabia*. Even now I can conjure up the image of us all sitting there in the gloom on our pillows watching Omar Sharif make that famous trek from the horizon to the well in one shot.

Peter O'Toole came from Hunslet and lived in the same street as my gran, Burton Street. I didn't know the family but from what I remember his mother always dressed in a Post Office uniform - trousers when women didn't wear trousers.
I've seen both of the cinemas great horses. Tom Mix's, Tony, and Roy Roger's, Silver.

Cinema has always provided a fine tradition in historical material. Although Hollywood's version of history has been more glamorous than anyone else's. Anyway, I remember realising that there might be more to life than heterosexuality when I saw Charlton Heston in *Ben Hur* on the big screen. I remember feeling turned on by the Roman soldiers in their togas and battledress with their complementary strong chests and thighs ...

I always bought *Photoplay*. I thought it was the most sophisticated film magazine in the world. I couldn't wait to get home and curl up in an armchair and follow up all the gossip about the stars. They really were stars. We had been denied any sort of glamour during and for some time after the Second World War. To read about the glittering lives of one's favourite film stars was such a treat but I never wrote a fan letter or belonged to a fan club. I think it had something to do with a fear of being rejected.

If Judy Garland had never sung *Somewhere Over The Rainbow* in *The Wizard of Oz*, then it's arguable that she may never have become the Patron Saint of gay men ... Friends of Dorothy, as we became known as. That song represents the gay quest in an era before so-called liberation. The truth was that Judy never found her rainbow, and of course there was the messy private life - the worthless men, the pills and booze, her seemingly endless ability to bounce back, resilient in the face of oppression. For gay men Judy was never more popular than when she was in decline - in *Meet Me In St Louis* the trolley might have gone clang, clang, clang, but Judy went rattle, rattle, rattle - and we loved her.

Then there's Miss Elizabeth Taylor, that rampant cleavage, all that camp larger-than-lifeness, all those men. Slugging it out with husband Richard in *Who's Afraid Of Virginia Woolf?* How her heart must have been broken (just like ours) when she fell in love with Jimmy Dean, Monty Clift and dear ol'Rock - gay boys to a man. Poor ol'Liz. God bless you, honey.

I once saw a film in which a person struck matches on their teeth. For weeks after I would steal matches in bulk and sneak away and try to light them. Not one lit. Another illusion popped.

I saw *Sayonara* when I was in the Navy. It was showing at the Takeraskatheatre in Yokohama. The film was about a Japanese girl who had her eyelids cut to make her eyes round like a western girl's. It made me think at the time about the kind of hold the western world had on the Japanese at that time. I mean you wouldn't get a western girl trying to make her eyes slanted.

A woman who smoked in the street used to be reckoned to be a bit of a tart and today one who does is reckoned to be a bit thick. It wasn't the case when I was young and although a lot of people reckon that smoking became acceptable because of freedoms which came about because of the War I reckon that a whole generation was turned on by the generation of smart starlets lighting up.

Watch any 1930s or 1940s film which isn't a costume drama and you'll see what I mean. The other night I counted the number of cigarettes that John Wayne smoked in *The Quiet Man*. He went through about sixty. He would always be opening packets and taking one out, then stubbing them out after a couple of puffs.

Like many of my generation, I knew little about our struggle for independence from Great Britain. *Gandhi* changed all that. I went to the Odeon on the third or fourth night and sat in an audience made up of all social groups and learnt about history. Up to that point I had never had any real desire to go back to my family roots. I was brought up in Kenya and Bradford, but that film made me want to go to India.

THE OSCARS

In 1927, in an attempt to raise the reputation of the film industry, tarnished after several scandals, the Academy Of Motion Pictures Arts and Sciences was founded. The Academy introduced annual achievement awards, the first being presented in May 1929.

The first ever Academy Award for best film went to *Wings*, an epic about fighter pilots in the First World War, starring the 'It' girl, Clara Bow. Until 1931 the Academy Award trophy was known simply as 'The Statuette'. A figure of a man standing on a reel of film, 13½ inches tall and covered in 10 carat gold plate, it was designed by Cedric Gibbons, the Art Director for MGM studios. The origin of the name 'Oscar' is attributed to the Academy Librarian, Margaret Herrick, who remarked on the statuette in 1931 that 'He looks like my Uncle Oscar'. The name stuck.

In 1946, the British Film Academy was founded, with similar aims as those of its American counterpart. Annual awards were given to the year's best British film, the first winner being *Odd Man Out* made in 1947, starring James Mason and Robert Newton. In 1968 the system of awards was reorganised and combined with Television awards.

61

Back in the fifties, when I was a lad and still in short trousers, I had the perfect introduction to the cinema. The first cinema I saw was mounted in a huge red removal van which had been converted to accommodate a mobile picture house complete with projector and speakers. On Saturday mornings the van would arrive, much to the excitement of myself and my friends.

A crowd of scruffy, ragged-arsed kids would gather as the cinema master climbed out of the van. He would produce a huge brass hand bell and proceed to wake the whole neighbourhood as he strutted up and down clanging it. After the collection box had been passed round and the required charge of tuppence had been got, the huge back doors were swung open to reveal a mass of wooden benches. The kids helped to remove the benches from the van and set them up. Inside the van, towards the middle, was a screen. Behind the screen was a projector and a loudspeaker. As far as I can remember the set-up was powered by a bank of batteries. I never saw a generator or anything like that.

The film would start up slowly and the music would sound awful until the projector had got up to the proper speed. The kids would roar with approval as Hoppalong Cassidy put his horse through its paces. Seeing as there was so much dust in the wake of this magnificent horse we could never figure out how Hoppalong always managed to look so smart all the time. He even found time to sing a song. The film used to break down a lot. The van came every week for about two years. Then it suddenly stopped. Someone said the man had suffered a heart attack when he found some creep had broken into the van and smashed the projector. I never did find out the reason he stopped coming. I know we all missed him for a while.

You don't use much film in physics teaching but for all of my life as a teacher the Tacoma Narrow Bridge break-up has been shown. It is a very early example of colour film but what makes it so spectacular is the way in which it demonstrates oscillation and structural defect. The wind caught the bridge and shook it until the complete structure broke into a wave motion. By any standards it is dramatic. The taking of the film was a complete accident but it has been used in so many classrooms that it must have been seen by more children in the world than have seen *Bambi*.

English audiences are so quiet. If you went into a back-yard cinema in Lagos then you would see a big difference. People like to partake in the film. It's like a football match really. Many of the films are martial arts films or Indian love stories. You identify with the goodies and the baddies, but you don't necessarily call them by those names. The hero is generally called The Actor.

Of course, there are also better quality cinemas such as The Super and The Odeon and then, for the professional classes, there is the National Theatre of Nigeria. That is where you will see the big American films.

If you go to the Kano Club Cinema in Nigeria then you take your own cushion because the stacking metal seats which you use can be very hard. The film itself is projected onto a concrete wall and the greatest hazard is flying insects. Of course when the wet season is on the film can come to an end because of rain. I never saw the end of *New York, New York* because I was running with the others for shelter.

Freetown, Sierra Leone, had two major cinemas in my youth; one was the Odeon and the other the Roxy. The Odeon was, as you would expect, built in the Odeon architectural style, that is, it was a 1930s building, not unlike the Government House, Fort Thornton. The Roxy came later and for a time vied with it for splendour. In those days cinema-going was a middle class occupation; you dressed up to go to the cinema and stood up at the end when they played the Queen. Later people got videos and it was not such a treat to go out to see films. Market lads got their enjoyment watching Kung Fu movies and Indian classics. I have never been sure what they made of the latter because many of them would have difficulty in reading any sub-titles that were there. I think it was the participation that they enjoyed and the larger-than-life pageant which passed before them. They didn't need to know much about subtleties of plots because everything focused on action rather than words.

Every national cinema has someone the little guys identify with and that makes their antics a box office success. In Europe it was Chaplin or Harpo Marx, in India, Raj Kapoor.

Going to a cinema in Holland is a serious business. It's so regimented, so officious. The ushers ensure that you keep quiet and there are none of the free and easy ways that you have in England.

The cinemas in Japan are totally different to British cinemas. The top job in a Japanese cinema is an usher. They don't have usherettes there, it's men who show you to your seat. The audience don't drop any litter, the cinemas are spotless and they show their appreciation by being quiet during the film. When the ice cream was served and there were gaps in the film they would talk about it and say how good or bad the film was.

For the first few days the waiters at the hotel we were staying in in Luxor were extremely polite. But on the fourth day they were stand-offish to the point of rudeness. This went on all day and by evening I was thoroughly fed up. I approached the manager and asked him why their attitude had changed.

'It's your T-shirt,' he said. 'They do not like the picture of Saddam Hussein.'

'Actually,' I said, 'that is a picture of my hero, Groucho Marx!'

Cinema- going has got to be the single most popular pastime in India. We stayed there for two months and for two months every Wednesday the man who ran the cafe at the top of Rattan bazaar in Old Delhi went to the pictures. Not just to see one film, but as many as he could fit in in one day. From what I could gather he was not unusual. A common thing to do on your day off is to go to the pictures all day.

I went a few times but found the pictures so badly cut by the censors that I found them hard to follow. One minute James Bond 007 was about to kiss the jewel in a belly dancer's navel, the next he was rolling arse over tit down a back alley with pursuers throwing dustbins at him.

When I was working in Iran in the late 70s my Iranian boyfriend said there was a fantastic American film showing in town that everyone was talking about. He was very excited and said I must have heard of it: *Fire in the Skyscratch*. I racked my brains but couldn't recall it. It wasn't until I got there that I saw the picture beneath the translated title, and realised they were showing *The Towering Inferno!*

In the late 60s and early 70s when I was in Tehran I used to go to the main cinema with my first wife. We used to watch all the western films and most of the Iranian women would try to copy the western ways from what they saw on the screen. Actually, most of it was a lot of rubbish, and it could cost you a lot of money as your wife would want a dress like this, or a coat like that. Sometimes it was better to go just with men.

We used to see films which mostly showed a poor boy getting involved with a girl from a rich family. The parents did not want the marriage to happen but, because they are really in love, after a lot of hassle and troubles, in the end they marry and there is a wedding. Everybody is happy, and of course we were all happy and smiling coming out of the cinema.

I used to go to the cinema mostly by myself. I took my mother once, but she wasn't very keen and it was expensive - about the equivalent of 5p - to look at a miserable face!

I was in Mashad, when I was a student. Of course, in a big town like Mashad there was a better cinema.

In Shirwan, Iran, where I came from, I went to the cinema for the first time when I was about seven years old in 1954. The cinema was a little place with no roof and we would go when it was dark and see black and white films. In Iran at night the stars can be beautiful. I can never get the same atmosphere in any cinema nowadays. It was so simple, but these multi-complex, or whatever you say, what are those? You might laugh at a cinema without a roof, but we loved it.

It was at t'Colli where I saw my first 3D Cowboy and Indian movie. Wearing those 3D red and green cardboard framed glasses was the latest craze. This particular day the Colli was packed and we'd arrived a little late. There were only seats left on the front row. We never used to sit on the front row, ever! But we sure got the 3D effect alright, those horses were coming right at us. We all slid down in our seats as much as we could and put our hands above our heads to protect ourselves.

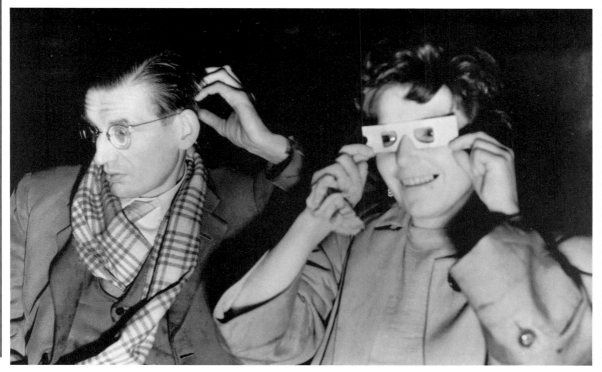

September was different. It was special, special, because I was going to the Odeon for my wedding reception.

Two wedding cars and a Leeds City Transport coach we had hired for the guests pulled up in front of the long queue of people waiting to go in. I swept past them all, white wedding gown and veil flowing. On past the pay box and on past the people waiting at the sweet kiosk buying their sweets and popcorn; still marching forward; bride, a groom, four bridesmaids, one page boy and twenty-six guests all fighting to go one way and the people coming out of the first showing all battling to go in the opposite direction.

There was a wonderful wide staircase that seemed to go upwards forever, at the top of which my new husband and I waited to greet our guests alongside a huge poster which said 'Kirk Douglas in *The Vikings* - Coming Soon.'

In the 60s if you wanted to go to the cinema and you were in a wheelchair you had to pre-book and could only go in the afternoon. There was no disabled access so you got manhandled up the stairs into the foyer and again into the theatre.

You were only allowed to sit at the end of a row near an exit and you had to transfer from your wheelchair into the cinema seat. The usherette then took your wheelchair away. They wouldn't let you see the film sitting in a wheelchair because you were a fire hazard but it was alright to sit in the cinema seat and burn to death.

It was a form of escapism from the dull routine life of most people. However, TV caught up with it and in two years reduced the number of operating cinemas from 4800 to 800. I know a man still involved in cinema management who told me that attendances are on the increase. But never again shall we hit the form it took in the 1940s and 50s.

I wonder if the kids today would be better off if we still had cinemas in every village? Mothers used to leave their kids whilst they went shopping and all the usherettes were called 'Aunty'.

Call it censorship if you like, but when the Phantom took his mask off at the Darfield Picture House, the manageress put up the lights so that the children would not be frightened.

The great thing about showing silent films was that since you didn't have to worry about any sound track, you could alter the length of time that they lasted. The standard projection speed was about sixty feet of film per minute. In practice you could speed things up considerably. If you wanted to get away early at the end of the night to catch your bus home you could make a one hour film last about fifty minutes. No-one ever seemed to notice or complain.

For the Saturday morning shows we used to hire entertainers to keep the kids amused in between films. We never seemed to have any trouble finding these people. In fact, we had a steady stream of people ready to work for nothing - frustrated stars who were happy just to have a chance to perform for an audience. This was their moment of glory and they were going to make the most of it. We had a very tight schedule to keep to and had to finish and get all the kids out in time for the first matinee show. Our biggest problem was these entertainers . Once they got out on stage some of them just wouldn't get off. I remember that once I had to open the window to the projection box and scream, 'Get off!'.

Items of ladies' underclothes, tanners, threepenny bits, half crowns, old music hall programmes, used FLs, old white fivers like sheets of paper, we found them all when we ripped out the carpets and turned old cinemas into bingo halls at the beginning of the 1960s. The carpets had to come up but it was horrible to see my mates tearing down beautiful plaster Roman pillars so that they could put up the big screens.

Many of the stall holders in Leeds Market used to make dogs and other animals from interwoven Woodbine cigarette packets. The models were always proudly displayed on high shelves above the poultry. They seemed to vie with each other as to who could create the most imaginative models.

Several years on, while watching the film, *Room At The Top* I saw one of these dogs being made. It was only a fleeting glimpse, Joe Lampton's uncle was interrupted in his interweaving to answer a knock at the door. Blink and you miss it ... like a lot of the minutiae which makes life interesting. I was quite excited - Im not sure why, a mixture of emotions I suppose - confirmation that such things had existed, a little thrill at seeing something which used to intrigue me as a child. The knowledge that that time period had been captured on film and wasn't completely gone. The film was black and white but my memory is turquoise/green, gold and black, white bloodstained overalls on plump ladies shouting prices for their plucked poultry.

Going to work on the bus, I used to pass the Wakefield Trinity rugby ground. When they were making the film *This Sporting Life* , big stuffed dummies started to appear on the terraces. As the days passed the terraces were getting more and more crowded with these huge dummies. I thought it looked ridiculous and that the film was going to be a silly one. When the film came out, I went to see it and I couldn't believe how realistic it looked. If you look carefully at the crowds in the match sequences, you can see that everybody is standing still except for a few men who are walking about to give the impression that it is a live crowd.

In our wisdom or otherwise we decided to show a sample film by the Westrex system to publicise the new installation. The complete range included a whispered conversation, the taps of Fred Astaire dancing, a full orchestra and finished with the El Alamein barrage as shown in the film *Desert Victory*.

To emphasise the range to its best effect it was possible to increase the volume and I instructed the chief operator to give the maximum when the barrage was being filmed. He did, and one evening after the end of the test film I walked into the circle foyer to find a man suffering from a mild form of shell shock. I asked him if there was anything we could do to help him and he then told me that he had participated in the actual battle and that he could never forget the sound of massed guns of every size as they opened up on that occasion for as far as the eye could see.

The first 'talkie' that I ever projected was *The Singing Fool*, starring Al Jolson. The sound for this came on gramophone records that you had to synchronise with the film. The secret was to make sure that the pictures and the sound started at exactly the same time. If you managed it first time you were lucky. If not, you had to go back to the beginning and start again, there was no way you could get it to match when the film was going.

For three weeks everything went perfectly and I suppose that I got a bit over-confident. One night I forgot to turn the record over when I changed projectors. I heard a roar of laughter from the audience and soon discovered the reason why. A man was singing with a woman's voice and vice versa. At one point, Al Jolson sang *Climb Upon My Knee Sonny Boy* over a shot of two people sitting in the back of a taxi.

THE TALKIES

The idea of combining sound with moving pictures is as old as the cinema itself. As early as 1896 audiences saw films accompanied by gramophone records and for the next three decades attempts were made to link the sound from gramophone records with events on the screen. The biggest problem was that of synchronisation. In the days when both cameras and projectors were hand-cranked it was almost impossible to achieve a perfect match of sound and vision.

In 1926 Warner Brothers bought the rights to a system which used a projector synchronised with wax gramophone discs. They christened this system 'Vitaphone'. It was this vitaphone system that was used for the most famous of the early talkies, *The Jazz Singer*, starring Al Jolson. *The Jazz Singer* opened on Broadway in October, 1927 and came to Britain the following year. Most of the sound sequences are made up of Jolson's songs but there are also a couple of short dialogue sequences. In total, three hundred and fifty-four words are spoken during the film.

Meanwhile, an alternative sound system where the sound track was recorded on the film itself, had been introduced. The first sound-on-film process had been patented by Eugene Lauste in 1906 and experiments had continued to improve his system. In 1928, Warner Bros released *The Lights of New York*, the first all-dialogue film, which used sound-on-film. The first feature-length talkie made in Britain was *Blackmail*, directed by Alfred Hitchcock, in 1929.

For a short time both systems, sound-on-disc and sound-on-film, operated in competition. Cinemas had to be equipped with projectors which were capable of showing films made with both. In the end, sound-on-film won the day because it was far less cumbersome and, more importantly, it did not have the problems of synchronisation which dogged Vitaphone.

❧A small gang of us were touring the country in a van demolishing everything. We were everywhere, Devon to Fifeshire, working as sub-contractors to Mecca. We altered Greens in the centre of Glasgow. That cinema was so big that it had three balconies and could hold thousands but we also dealt with the little cinemas, places built in villages and called names like The Electric.

The money was to be made off expenses for although we got reasonable pay there was an extra thirty bob accommodation money to be claimed even if we slept, as we usually did, in the back of the van. What we didn't do was try to sell what we found. That's a pity because I now see some of those items at collectors fairs. An old cinema ticket from the 1930s can fetch over £100 today. I've put thousands in the skip.

❧ It's sad when a picture house becomes something else. Between Chapeltown and the Harrogate Road there's an elegant 1930s building which has a Star of David in the ornamental iron work. Locals call it the *Cinemagogue*.

❧ The Grange is a do-it-yourself place up Thornton Road way but if you look carefully you'll see on the roof the flues for the two arc lamps. I've thought of asking the wife if she'll get me one for Christmas so that I can put it onto our roof at home.

I was the projectionist there and at the Marlborough; that's now a warehouse. Only the Plaza - opened in 1913 - another place that employed me, is still in the business of entertaining people. That's now open for bingo.

One day, I was walking home from work when a motorist stopped and asked me directions. I said, 'Continue down this road to the main road, turn left and it's about a hundred yards up past the Rialto on your left.'

As the motorist drove off I realised the Rialto had been closed for at least ten years! It didn't close to become a bingo hall but a firm of engineers took it over. For a few years after the engineers had moved in, the only change they made to the exterior of the front of the house was to add the word 'Works' to Rialto. They used a side entrance and kept the foyer boarded behind the iron concertina gates.

Gradually, all the ornamentation of fake wooden pillars began to rot. Cracks became posting holes for things to be pushed into their hollow interiors. All my school mates from the next village used to wait for their bus outside the Rialto Works.

Someone started a craze for posting pre-decimal ha'pennies into one of those decaying pillars. The idea caught hold and everyone did it. Every day, any old ha'pennies would be stuffed into this money box.

❧ The Tower, Arcadian, Sangeet, Marlborough, Essoldo and Royal, they all showed Indian films all of the time. There was a wonderful choice, though there were queues. When a blockbuster came along you needed tickets, but if you couldn't get them then you moved on to another cinema. There was such a choice.

All sections of the community went, Hindus, Moslems, Sikhs, Christians; all ages, all social groups. The language was Hindustani but everyone understood, and subtitles were not needed. Indian films are not films without a song but, unlike English ones, the style of one piece does not interfere with the style of the next. Indian classical music gets linked in with disco numbers.

Of course, many of the plots are straight forward and traditional, taken from the Mahabharata or the Ramayana. There are revenge stories in which twins get separated, then reappear. Or social dramas in which a poor guy is hassled by a rich one. Occasionally we would see a controversial film which was banned in India, such as *Shaan* or *Mother Country*, a film which showed the problems of young people coming to terms with living an Indian cultural life in London.

It seemed that Indian cinema would go on forever then, overnight, along came the video shop and, within a couple of years, all the cinemas were empty.

People wouldn't accept that the Odeon had come down. A good year after it had been levelled people would ring.

'Hello. Can you tell me what's on tonight?'

'We knocked the cinema down last June.'

'You can't have done. I passed it only last week and it was there.'

'The area's flat'

'How come then that you are there?'

'I'm sitting in a portacabin at the centre of a building site.'

Our cinema had the biggest read-o-graph in the North, a great screen almost the size of half a tennis court which stood above the canopy. The letters we attached to it to advertise the current film were almost two feet high.

When we made the decision to rebuild as a cinema complex we collapsed the building from the back and to maintain a presence in Barkers Pool, put up the message 'Goodbye Sheffield, We Will Return in 1985. Thank You For Your Custom.'

What we hadn't reckoned with was the high spirits of the builders. They found a cut-out of Michelangelo's David. Did something with his dangly bits and hoisted him up onto the advertising screen. Then they rearranged the letters. You can make quite a few obscenities from a message thanking your customers for their support.

In the late 1950s you could pick up a cinema organ for next to nothing. If you paid £250 you were touching top price. Remember, no-one needed them. Size, for one thing was a problem because although the console - the bit you see - is compact enough, it is the sound chamber with all the pipes, glockenspiel, bass drum, snare drum and xylophone which take up a lot of space. They are not like computers.

Now you would be lucky to get one for less than £50,000, but, with so many enthusiasts, men are prepared to build extensions on their houses for British Comptons and American Wurlitzers.

Audience participation is all well and good if you're in the mood. I think that is generally agreed. Now put yourself in my position. I was dragged from the comfort of a public house to watch a late night screening of that cursed film *The Rocky Horror Picture Show* to find a cinema full of high-spirited people in fancy dress. At that time of my life these sort of folk were the sworn enemy.

I was from the rough part of the district, so had the reputation amongst my college friends of being a real thug. As the singing and swaying and jumping up and down continued all around me I was uncontent, rigid and arms folded. Something had to give and when a young Gothic held a candle above my head spilling wax into my hair my reputation was soon transferred into legend.

I was never keen to be out in London at night on my own but I had to go to see *Psycho*. When I arrived at the cinema it was like nothing I had ever seen before. The scale of everything was enormous, the whole interior was palatial with marble columns and a good imitation of the hanging gardens of Babylon. I think there was even a fountain in the foyer. It took me ages to find where to buy my ticket. The cinema itself was like a Busby Berkley film set except there was no one around. I had the floor to myself and it was scary. The staircase seemed a long way off. I felt there were unseen eyes watching me from behind the plants. Uniformed ushers at unexpected junctions of corridors and staircases unsmilingly pointed me in the right direction. I was terrified of getting lost. Finally, I was ushered by torch-light to my seat in the vast auditorium; the film had already started. I regained my composure, watched the action and wondered what all the fuss was about it being a scary film. The shower scene was nothing to the ordeal I had been through just getting there.

When we arrived, things were a bit odd from the start. The ticket girl, a pretty blonde, gave me, slowly and deliberately, eight pound coins as change from a five pound note. I tried to explain, I really did, but she just smiled and pushed the coins back to me. Fair enough, so we bought some popcorn with the windfall. The blonde girl ran the snack bar as well as the ticket office and left the guy behind us who was waiting to buy tickets to serve us. On turning to the stairs we were greeted by the ticket collector: 'Hello there, how are you? We haven't seen you two since,

err.. November wasn't it?' he boomed.
'Can't remember what it was you watched, *Die Hard II*..No..?'
The novel concept of memorising your customers and the films they watch was marred only by the fact that neither of us had ever been there before!

This tall, grey, slightly scruffy man was also the projectionist, we learnt. In fact the whole enterprise was apparently run by just the two of them.

The cinema itself is one of those mock-deco mausoleums with plaster trellises and huge lilies everywhere and lighting which can't quite make it to the corners. I can remember that there was a glorious clock on the wall, a bronze Mucha-inspired figurine pointing out the appropriate time on a dial of leaves. Bloody difficult to tell what time it was but a lot of fun working it out.

All that opulence was strangely out of keeping with the building site below the balcony. From the bottom of the screen as far as the eye could see were piles of bricks, mounds of sand, the odd cement mixer and various trowels. Renovation.

This is a big old place, not like the smaller studios being built now but there were rows and rows of empty seats. The bloke behind us at the ticket booth far off on the left and another couple way at the back, lots of arms and legs but all entwined together.

As the lights dimmed the prettyish blonde made her way to the front right in front of us and stood in an awkward, embarassed silence. I had a nagging suspicion that she'd be better off stopping at the three groups and asking if they wanted anything rather than standing right at the front looking neither left or right. We decided to buy a choc ice from her out of pity.

❧ I don't get the same kick out of a visit to the cinema these days. We went to see *The Unforgiven* at The Showcase in Leeds but the film was an hour too long. Despite the comfortable seating and the large container of popcorn, the atmosphere of magic and anticipation was missing.

The place was clean, big and functional but market forces have no place in the world of art and films. Cinema is a high art form sadly neglected in this country. We used to be a world leader in this area but like any of our other big industries, if you starve them of resources they contract and then they die.

❧ These days, I wait until films come out on video. It is not the same. There is no build-up and no feeling of communicating with people of like minds.

I'm glad that I lived through the days when stars were put on a pedestal. They were magical and untouchable creatures, created for us to admire and adore. Grooming stars was a big business but somehow they kept their mystique and that is what is missing in today's world cinema.

We always made a detour to the fish shop on the way home from the pictures. Eating fish and chips out of newspaper and talking about the film was all part and parcel of the night out. We can't turn the clock back now. How I wish that we could.

❧ When my dad came out of the Imax in Bradford he turned to me and said, 'Think of that. A working man should have lived to see something as wonderful as that.'

I could see what he meant. Hollywood didn't exist in any real sense when he was born in 1909.

The only skill needed to be
an usherette is to be able to walk backwards,
upstairs, in the pitch dark and to sell
ice cream in total silence.

CHAPTER FOUR

WE STARTED WORK
WHEN EVERYONE
ELSE FINISHED

People don't realise the number of staff that a big cinema would employ. When I worked at the New Victoria in the 1930s, we had a staff of about a hundred. There were six entrances to the auditorium, each of which had its team of usherettes - we had about forty usherettes. Plus, of course, all the box office and sales staff. Then there was the manager, his assistant and all the office staff, and six projectionists and their assistants. When you add on all the cleaners and people like the lift boys, electrician, and the man who looked after the boiler room, you get some idea of the number of people needed to operate a big cinema.

We were opposite to other workers as we didn't start work until about one o'clock in the afternoon and we worked through until about nine o'clock at night. Our social life was nil.

The uniform looked very formal and grand with gold braid on the lapels and epaulettes, but really this was just an illusion. What it was, was an overall wrapped over at the front and tied with straps at the back, just an illusion to dazzle.

In fact, just like the cinema.

My two main ambitions as a child were simple. I wanted to be an usherette in a cinema or to serve behind the counter in Woolworth's.

The organist's appearance on the rising organ - all flashing lights and transparent bakelite - was a magic moment. But for all that he usually went down to a barrage of orange peel.

Getting the job at the Odeon in Portsmouth was wonderful. My duties were to show patrons to their seats, deal with tickets, sell ice cream and keep a check on vacant seats so that the front of house staff could control the queue of people.

I loved it! Fancy being paid to do something you enjoyed so much! I was so starry-eyed at the big screen that I frequently lost patrons. They were supposed to be following

STAFF.
'Nothing will help so much to secure regular patrons, with a consequent levelling up of the box office receipts, as the exercise of care and discretion in the appointment of the theatre staff. From the manager downwards, the employees should be selected quite as much for their personal character as for their business capacity. The desideratum is to get hold of the right people, for they are those who are going to make your house a popular resort, or a place to be fought shy of and avoided.'

How To Run A Picture Theatre, 1911

behind me to take their seats in the appropriate row but quite often people would sneak into the more expensive seats and I would be left high and dry. The only hope of finding the cheats was to slowly retrace my steps and shine my chunky torch in everyone's face. I didn't bother after the first few times because the light irritated the genuine patrons and there wasn't a cat in hell's chance that I would recognise them. Besides, I wouldn't have had a clue what to say to them if I had caught anyone.

I could count on the fingers of one hand the number of times that I had been to the cinema before I went to work as an usherette. Suddenly it was like magic, like going to the theatre. I remember the name of the first film I saw. It was *The Woman In The Window*, starring Edward G. Robinson. I was so fascinated by the film that I kept forgetting to take people's tickets. When you are an usherette you don't see a film through - just little bits. It took four showings for me to get the whole story.

The manager was not enchanted with me. He ordered me to his office where he had my cards and a week's wages ready on his desk.

'Miss Copworth' (Cawthorne, he never could get my name right) 'I have had complaints from patrons who tell me that you drape yourself over the back stalls and recite all the speeches from the film. Take your wages and your cards and get out of here.'

I once took my children to a cinema party. Leaving three very well-behaved, quiet children in the care of the usherette, off I went to enjoy a rare taste of freedom. I returned a couple of hours later to pick them up.

The sight that met my eyes was unbelievable. The films were over and a singer was struggling on the stage to entertain the packed house. No one could possibly have heard her voice. Both my boys were fighting like mad but, for once, not with each other. In fact, most of the children were rolling about in their seats and some in the aisles. The whole cinema shook with a noisy uproar, every child participating.

I said to the usherette, 'How on earth are you going to get this lot out?'

She said , 'Don't worry - watch this' .

The manager was coming from the back of the cinema to climb onto the stage. He roared through the microphone, 'There will be liquorice allsorts for every child at the exit on your way out.'

The place was emptied in a remarkably short time. The usherettes were almost trampled to death.

I never did find out if there were enough sweets provided to go round as I had to fight against a tide of frantic children to find my youngest son's coat which, by now, only had one sleeve.

He wore a better uniform than a five star general. He was the one who kept the queue in order and fed us cinema-goers through the correct doors. By the time I became an usherette, that job had disappeared, or was done by the cinema manager in a dark-suit.

During one matinee, Olive lost control. She leapt on the stage, waved her torch about like a searchlight and yelled: 'You might all go t'Gospel Hall and sing *Stand Up, Stand Up, For Jesus* but when you're in here it's for Christ's sake, sit down! And where are you going?'

'To lav, miss,'

'Sit down and hold it!'

This last comment was accompanied by a tap on the head with her torch.

THE USHERS

'The attendants who show people to their seats can help you to make friends or they can drive trade away. You want bright youths or young women who are willing to work and whom you can trust to do as well when you are absent as when you are there. Part of their duties should be to keep the house tidy while it is open. If they do this and give proper care to the seating of the new arrivals, they will not have much time for flirting but if they exhibit a tendency in that direction, warn them that a repetition of the offence will act as an automatic dismissal, and stick to it. Nothing hurts a house more than gossipy attendants.'

How To Run A Picture Theatre, 1911

Once inside it was pitch dark and unless an usherette was available with a torch you stumbled about trying to find your seat. You then had to get rid of all your outer clothing and store it under your seat. My dad once got settled and then began helping himself to toffees from Mam's lap until he received a hard slap on the hand and found that he wasn't sitting next to Mam at all.

We had lots of films about people being lost in the desert. On those nights the manager would tell the projectionist to turn the heating up because this would mean an increase in the sale of ice cream. I know it's laughable, but it worked. You see, the manager and the sales girls earned commission. We usually took it in turns to sell ice cream and in that way earned a few extra shillings.

In northern towns there was always an interval when a uniformed young lady with a maid's cap and apron would walk round and up and down the aisles holding on high a spray from which issued clouds of sweetly-scented disinfectant.

I was working at the Empire as an usherette and only took the job to augment my income. I was a student nursery nurse earning next to nothing.

One evening Mr Hyam, the manager, called me to his office.

'Why is it young lady, that your torch batteries don't last as long as everyone elses?'

I looked up at him with innocent brown eyes.

'I don't know, Mr Hyam,' I said. 'I really don't know.'

But there was a good reason. One evening he caught me red-handed doing my homework by torchlight. I thought he had gone to catch his bus and that the coast was clear but he'd slipped back for some reason. He never questioned me about the life span of my torch batteries again and turned a blind eye if he ever caught me doing my homework by torchlight.

I remember an occasion when my mum took me to the pictures. As we were going into the auditorium my mum let out a scream. The usherette had slipped when she was putting our tickets on to a long metal spike and the spike had stuck into my mother's hand. She was so badly hurt that we ended up going back home instead of staying for the film.

My job was to catch anyone sneaking into the cinema without paying. If I managed it I got five shillings reward.

By this time I was about fourteen, really grown up. Well, this chap, Nash, came up to me, gave me his ticket and I tore it in half. Then I looked closely and realised it was an old one, out of date. By this time he had gone in, but I followed and asked the usherette where he was sitting. She took me to him and I said, 'Out!' I got my five shillings.

It must have been eight or nine years later when I was courting and I took Ursula to a cinema in the next town. We bought two tickets. Times had changed and there, standing taking the tickets, was this chap Nash, now a commissionnaire.

He tore my tickets, looked at me and said, 'If ever you come again, don't worry about paying, I'll let you in.'

Ursula said to me, 'Isn't that nice of him!'

I said, 'No way. I always pay my way.'

I thought, 'I've caught him once, I'm not going to let him catch me!'

The unseen, unsung maestro of the cinema staff was the chief operator. He was a man of many parts being a skilled electrician, a showman, familiar with the complicated machinery of a projector and capable of understanding the mercury arc rectifier which turned alternating current into direct current.

When a film arrived for showing it was packed in reverse order of showing in round cartridges of about 600 feet. Two parts were fastened together by amyl acetate for loading into the projector. He was expected to examine the film to ensure it wasn't oily or scratched and that the joints were good to eliminate the risk of the film breaking whilst being shown. He had to be certain that all the film had been delivered and then to arrange the running order. His responsibilities also included seeing that secondary lighting was lit before the cinema lights were dimmed, checking that his staff was capable of running the projectors and being certain that the dialogue was synchronised with the film.

He was paid above the average wage because of his responsibilities and for the unsocial hours he was expected to work. Most cinema staff were dedicated to their jobs. If not they left.

THE OPERATOR

'You can build a sumptious theatre, furnish and decorate it with a lavish hand, and drag the people in by force if you will, but unless the picture is properly projected you will never fill your theatre day after day and week after week. Remember what 'makes the show': some reels of film, a machine, and - the operator. Without the latter there would be no show. He never has his name in big letters in front of the house. His name is sometimes not even known by the other employees of the place. To them he is simply and only 'the operator', but nevertheless, when it comes to giving credit where credit is due, if the show is what it should be, don't forget the man up there in the coop - the man behind the gun.'

How To Run A Picture Theatre, 1911

We were told regularly at daily inspection that we were all part of the J. Arthur Rank Organisation and had its good name to uphold, so woe betide anyone who wasn't smart and proud to wear their uniform. I truly can't remember anyone who wasn't, although we were a motley lot. There was a mirror in both dressing rooms. We checked our appearance under a quotation which said 'Personal appearance is all-important.' Totally in awe, we believed anything, and all this for the princely sum of fifteen shillings per week. We jumped to it whenever we were told.

Every evening, fifteen minutes before we opened the doors, we had a staff inspection. All of us would be lined up in the foyer, waiting for the manager. The manager would then walk up and down the line checking our appearance. First, we had to hold our hands out in front of us so that he could see that our hands and fingernails were clean. Then he would walk behind us and check that the seams on the women's stockings were straight. There was a very strict dress code for all members of staff - except for the projectionists. They were allowed to come to work dressed in whatever they wanted.

THE MANAGER

'He should be a man of methodical business habits, quick at feeling the pulse of the public, but above all, one who can make himself popular with all he habitues of the place. Many a proprietor owes his success to his manager's personality. Kindly consideration and personal attention count for a great deal. The public like to go to a place of entertainment where the manager evinces a personal interest in them, and they are not slow to resent any stand-offishness displayed by the man in authority. Civility, pleasantness, and an evident desire to please should always be exercised...The manager is the one who is really in charge of the program of the theatre, and upon him depends to some extent both the pleasure of the patrons and the profit of the owner.'

How To Run A Picture Theatre, 1911

Mr Rowe, the manager, and his family came from London and at first he and his nineteen-year-old daughter, Miriam, ran the projection room. Shortly afterwards, a boy in the class above me at school was taken on as assistant to relieve the manager. I still remember how envious I felt at this boy being given such an opportunity. When this boy left school and started work, his place was taken by my best friend, Colin, some months older than me. After a while the manager decided to employ another schoolboy assistant, presumably to save money on wages. My friend recommended me and I duly presented myself at five-thirty on that first Monday evening full of excitement and enthusiasm and just thirteen years of age.

❧ During the war I was a page boy at the Commodore Cinema just outside Slough. It was more like a commissionaire and although I was just thirteen years old I was doing a man's job. I had a bottle green uniform with military style cap, gold braid and coat tails, but since all the men had gone to war, or were in the forces, I didn't look that strange.

The queue for the last house stretched for about three hundred yards and was six deep. One night I was standing by the main door to take the tickets and this soldier dropped some cash. A half-crown rolled straight towards me and went under my foot. Everyone around was looking for it, but I just kept my legs still, though feeling really guilty. This was a lot of money to me as I was only getting fifteen shillings a week. For a time I wrestled with my conscience and then said, 'Excuse me sir, it's here,' and went to give it back to him. He looked at me and said, 'You keep it son, for being honest.' That was a good lesson for a thirteen-year-old.

❧ Some tell me that if you look closely you can see a red sports car in *Ben Hur*. I don't know about that but as a projectionist, watching films night after night, you develop an eye for detail.

A film came on the television only the other night. I said to the wife, 'If you look closely at the sky above the nineteenth century steam locomotive you'll see jet vapour trails.' Sure enough, we saw them.

❧ The projectors were the latest BTH (British Thompson Houston) machines lit by carbon arc, an extremely bright light, only to be viewed through the coloured glass peephole in the side of the projector. Besides showing films, the projectors were adapted to show advertising slides during the intervals or urgent messages during the performances. The only other equipment in the room was a twin turntable with a selection of popular records used to provide music before the films started. There was a selection of military marches played at the end of the shows while the patrons were leaving. The one currently being played when I started was *Blaze Away* but, being nautically minded, I seem to remember changing it to *On The Quarterdeck*.

❧Laurence Harvey and Olivia Hussey in the film of *Romeo and Juliet* was my first introduction to Shakespeare. Up until then he had always mystified me. I learnt the whole thing by heart, as it was retained for three weeks. I saw it seventy-two times.

❧During my first week as a projectionist the film showing was the musical *New Moon*. It was in black and white as were most films at the time. It was a longer than usual feature and instead of the programme changing mid week, as normal, *New Moon* was showing twice nightly, Monday to Saturday. By the end of the first week I felt as though I knew the script backwards and was wondering if I had made the right decision. Was it going to be too monotonous? Would the constant whirring of the projectors get on my nerves and could I stand spending five hours every evening and Saturday afternoons cooped up in the projection room, especially during the summer? Time alone would tell.

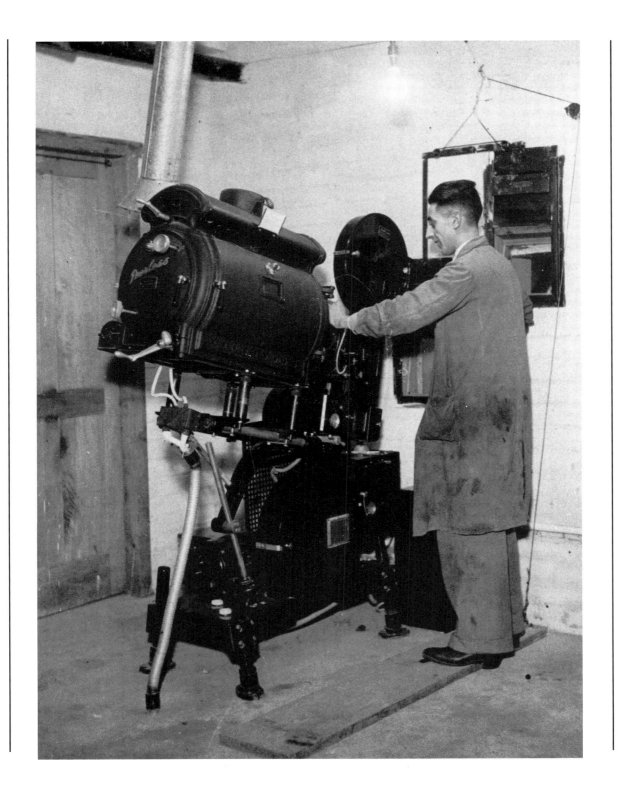

In those days I was very keen on trains and I heard that a church hall in Streatham was showing a programme given by the LMS - to my mind the London, Midland and Scottish Railway. I turned up in good time to get the best seat. To my great surprise the films were all about native Africans and Indians - not a thing about trains. My religious knowledge was so scant in those days that I did not know that LMS stood for the London Missionary Society.

There was an art in changing from one spool to another without the audience noticing. Shortly before the end of a spool a set of dots would appear on the top right hand corner of the film. On seeing the first set of dots the second machine was set running, the first few feet of film being the leader. Each machine had a set of spring-loaded shutters over the gate which were opened or closed by twisting a handle. On observing the second set of dots on the screen the handles were twisted together so that as one gate was closed the other was opened and, all things being equal, the reels were changed without the slightest hitch in the viewing. Normally two operators would effect the change over but with experience standing in between the machines using both hands, one on each gate, a perfect change over could be made by just one operator.

There's a line in one of the great horror films which always comes to me when I think of those early projection rooms. A kite is flying in the air high above Frankenstein's workshop. The monster, or is it the Bride, is on the slab surrounded by antiquated equipment, spools are whirling.
'Throw the switch, Igor. The storm is almost overhead.'

Every Monday and Thursday afternoon, films were delivered to the cinema by General Film Distributors. Each reel of ten minutes' duration came in round tin boxes called cans, duly labelled with the name of the film and reel number. All the cans travelled in a fireproof metal chest. With all the thousands of feet of highly inflammable celluloid, fire safety was of the utmost importance.

The spools used on the projector took twenty minutes of film so before the first performance on Mondays and Thursdays the programme had to be *made up*. Two reels of film had to be wound onto a twenty minute spool and joined in the middle so that there was no break. The spools were then numbered and placed in the rack in order of showing. As the spools came off the machine they had to be rewound onto a spare spool and placed back in the correct slot in the rack ready for the next performance.

My first month was spent rewinding the films, learning how to make joins and mend breaks using a clear acetate glue which smelt of, and resembled, nail varnish. I also learnt how to operate the turntable and show advertising slides during the intervals.

I got a taste for bits of film when I used to splice them out of reels which arrived at the cinema when I was working as a boy projectionist. That interest has gone on. I would take a foot at a time and make magic lantern slides but now I buy what I can afford. There's really quite a trade in buying and selling old movies. Sometimes I get given old stock containing surprises. Recently I found among what I thought was a load of junk some excellent footage of the building of the Regal Cinema in Hull in 1933. I've also had films on aircraft recognition and old Gas Board films.

My problem is that I can't resist a bargain. I've already got twenty Bell and Howell 16 mm projectors but I still can't resist sneaking another one in without my wife knowing.

During the early part of my working life I worked for a film distributor in Leeds called Monarch Films. Despite my junior position, I felt partly responsible for the quality of the films we handled. Me and a friend once went to the Clock at the bottom of Roundhay Road when up on the screen it flashed *Arctic Adventure*.
'Oh no. It's one of ours', I confessed, burying my head in my hands. It was one of those shorts they used to show before the main feature but the problem was it wasn't short enough. On and on it bloody well went. You couldn't see a damn thing for the blizzard blowing and all you could hear in the background was a dreadful monotone commentary. The firm folded shortly afterwards.

You had to book months ahead to see *Hamlet* at the Scala. Somehow I managed to book a ticket for the day I had two teeth out at the dentist.

Before I went in I bought a half pound pack of cotton wool. By the end of the film I'd gone through the lot. What the cleaners made of the mess I'd left under the seat, I can't imagine.

Four days after leaving school I started work as a pageboy at the Plaza Cinema, Queensbury, Middlesex, for ten shillings a week. It was Boxing Day, 1938 and a Sunday. I couldn't start work quickly enough. The first main feature film for the week starting Monday was Anna Neagle in *Sixty Glorious Years* and my friends thought it was a good omen for a long cinema career. I worked from nine in the morning until nine in the evening every day with an hour for lunch and an hour for tea. My main morning task was clearing out two thousand ash trays in the seats. I have never liked cigarettes since. On my day off, Tuesday, I went to the other town cinema.

The Odeon, Headrow, had a ghost. All the cleaners knew that but I had never seen it until the night Mary Gledhill and I were locking up the little room at the top of the cinema. I said, 'Look,' and there she was, standing in front of a mirror titivating her hair, yet there was no reflection. We were down those stairs like we'd been shot at. The rest laughed. They'd seen her before.

As cleaners, we found a lot of things in the rows - especially one thing you eat and one thing you play with. But I have also seen other things. For instance, I've seen three mice who we called Mickey, Minnie and Mate. They used to come out to watch us clean.

A rugby injury had left Ted with a flattened, twisted nose, although he somehow still remained fairly good looking. Ted was tailor-made for playing baddies but rarely got the chance until they did a remake of *Flash Gordon* in 1979.

All the pub-goers in Ilkley turned out for that one. Not only was he a baddie, he was their leader. It was very strange seeing the bloke who ten minutes before had served me with a half of bitter swooping through the infinity of space at twice the speed of light.

A few years ago we got involved with a company called Sound and Vision. They bought in advertising films which were disguised as documentaries and I toured them round Women's Institutes and old folks' homes. I had an area and had to make so many bookings each year. The films included one made by Heinz about their product, another about the joys of Eastbourne and *Home Is Where The Heat Is*. This was about the joys of calor gas.

It's hard to see what people got out of them except the pleasure of sitting in a darkened room and being together. It was a social occasion, very different from watching video. Usually they had a raffle. Once I won a tin of peaches.

There was always a mystique about the cinema. The sheer thrill when the lights are lowered and the curtains drawn aside to show the first frames of the censor's certificate is magic. I often sit in the front of the stalls looking back up into the projection box where the pinpoint beam begins and widens into the full width of the screen. The cinema still thrills me.

Just after the First War, when the managers and owners were consolidating their position, my uncle would take himself off to meetings of the Cinematographic Association in France. He'd always come back with something. One year he bought my aunt a fox fur as a present.

Everybody over there, he said, enjoyed his company because each year he would regale that august assembly with his rendition of *On Ilkley Moor Ba T'at*.

Every night the owner would sit at the back and watch the audience. When he came out he would say to me, 'There's £110 in there tonight.' Remember, that was in the years when the cheap seats were 6d and the dear ones 1/3d. He was rarely out by more than a pound.

I applied for a job I had seen advertised in the local *Express* for a management trainee with an independent cinema circuit and was lucky. I spent three months in head office learning the system of administration then three months in the operating box of a local cinema to learn about presentation. I was then attached to a senior cinema manager to complete the course. It was all about staff control and training, controlling queues and keeping a good image in the entrance hall by wearing a dinner jacket. I remember the first time I wore a DJ. I thought I had ten pairs of hands and just didn't know what to do with them. Eventually, by custom, it became just a uniform. The final piece of advice I had from my instructor was, 'Don't fiddle the petty cash or get involved with any of the female staff. There's more men walking the Thames Embankment because of these two faults than any other.'

There were a lot of in-house romances. Only to be expected really, given the mix of young men and women and the unsocial hours that we worked. The manager didn't mind so long as we didn't let it interfere with our work and we only socialised when we were off duty. I met my wife when she was an usherette and I was a projectionist. After we were married she worked with me in the projection box for several years when my usual assistant was serving in the army.

The manager at the Beaufort in Ward End had everything going against him. He was effeminate, and I mean effeminate, and yet he was definitely one of the most exciting and original men I have ever come across. It was nothing to see him rush down the aisle, sing a song or two and then rush back again. He did that at the silent screening of *Show Boat*. During the interval of *Rose Marie* he and his wife erected a wigwam and sang songs from the show.

Once he had a funny week. He had bill-stickers put the posters upside down and showed the Laurel and Hardy film that way too.

❧There wasn't much for film stars to do in Birmingham so they often brought them down to General Advertising to see how we did their posters. That's how I met Chico and Harpo Marx, and Laurel and Hardy. That would be in 1930, just before the talkies.

I was responsible for doing both the Art Posters, cards in watercolour which went in the foyer, and also the big West End posters. These measured twenty feet by ten feet and got pasted up around the city centre. It seemed strange that big stars like these should be interested in this type of work but then I suppose they were pretty average men when you think of it. They were just fabulously rich in a poster writer's terms.

Mind you, cinema poster writers were always badly paid. As a fully-fledged poster artist I was getting just fifteen shillings a week.

❧ I saw Stan Laurel and Oliver Hardy when they came to Bradford but it was hard to equate them with the films. The first thing that you noticed about Oliver Hardy was his big red face - a feature naturally lost on a black and white film. Stan Laurel was a little old man in a trilby, quiet and ordinary looking, so it's amazing to see that there is a museum devoted to his memory at Ulverston. People who were not even born when they were alive can do imitations. One movement, such as the twiddling of the tie, causes everyone in the world to know exactly who they are pretending to be.

They have their devotees to this day. A customer of mine, who deals in silk screen equipment, calls his firm *Another Fine Mesh*.

❧ Mr Hyam was the manager of the Empire in Airedale during the forties. He was a retired stage artiste whose professional name was *The Great Hyam*. He had spent his stage life as a stand-up comic which was obvious by his manner and posture. When the film broke down, which it invariably did, he would put the house lights up and walk sedately down the aisle. Stopping half-way, he would call out in a solemn voice, 'We will now sing hymn number twenty seven.' He also always played light classical music before the film started and during breakdowns. It was only after he retired that modern music, or music relating to the film, was played.

❧ In the 1940s, even in cinemas in poor districts, the manager always stood in the foyer and welcomed customers as if they were guests. People appreciated this because you have to see that going to the pictures was a social event, something that took you out of the routine. That's why some families went twice weekly.

This atmosphere allowed the manager to be influential in the way he managed his house. He was his own man and no cinema in an area showed the same film because managers were responsible for their own programmes and, in some areas, their own publicity. As a consequence, managers developed their own style. Leslie Holderness, manager of the Paramount, New Street, for instance, had seven shrunken heads in his office and Gene Autry's cowboy hat.

❧ I remember during one evening performance an usherette came to tell me that a young woman had fainted in the stalls. I went into the darkened auditorium and there was this young lady out to the world. I told the usherette to get a chair from my office and put it in the foyer. When I got her out onto the chair I asked the young man with her if she suffered from fainting fits and was told that, as she was due to have a baby, she had started passing out. I learned the baby was due that weekend - it was Friday I was lucky in having two women on my staff who were in their forties, they had seen it all before and were able to cope with the situation. I rang for a taxi, all the time keeping my fingers crossed, and breathed a sigh of relief when it left with the almost completed family. The sequel came about two weeks later when one of the staff announced there was a young man to see me. I didn't recognise him, but, when he referred to the instance of the pregnant woman, I realised it was the husband. He thanked me for helping out and asked me my Christian name. His wife wanted to name the baby after me.

I had the good luck to enter the cinema business when it was respectable. It was possible to go with parents, children, even grandparents without any fear of being embarrassed. There were no full frontals, the film censors saw to that, there was no great violence and no science fiction films.

A young man requested me to put a slide on the screen asking for a man in the audience to come to the entrance. I asked if it was important as, for obvious reasons, I didn't want to interrupt the programme. He replied, 'T'winds blown roof off his bloody house. Is that important enough?' The slide went on.

The manager was always taking me to task for varying the records I played in the interval. There was a large and up-to-date selection to go at and I used to play them to suit myself, regardless of the audience. What I didn't realise was that each time a record was played it had to be recorded on a form by the manager so that royalties could be paid. Varying the programme of records, instead of repeating the same two or three, meant extra paperwork and cost. This wasn't appreciated.

As I worked my way up from an usherette to a cashier, I became aware that this was as far as women could go. All the managers were male. Maybe they didn't think a woman could wear an evening suit. If you became head cashier you were really the manager's second wife, or rather, the manager's dogsbody.

THE BOX OFFICE ATTENDANT

'It is best to put a woman in charge of the box office, partly because women are apt to be more reliable, and in part because they ask less money. You want one who is pleasant and who can smile as she hands out the change. One who is not too old to be attractive, and one who is steady enough to refuse the numerous opportunities for flirtation will become an asset. She should be alert to her business, and should make every sale in a manner which conveys the impression that the patron confers a favour in asking for a ticket.'

How To Run A Picture Theatre, 1911

The only skill needed to be an usherette is to be able to walk backwards up steps in the pitch dark and to sell ice cream in total silence.

One of the tricks was for two of you to go in early and open the emergency doors to let in the rest of the gang. Once I remember a manager storming up to the front and saying, 'There's summat wrong here, I've only taken two bob and the place is full.'

One of the advantages of having a number of screens is that you can respond to popular taste and bring a film back for just one night. *The Exorcist* has been round for twenty-five years but we can buy it in and, if it is well advertised, guarantee an audience.

Total Recall was a man's film. The cinema was full and out of the four hundred seats there would be no more than ten women. Two of these were seated at the back accompanied by a little man and one at the front with a big man. I had just gone out to settle some details about a benevolent fund, which we had got caught up with, when the usherette came

THE DOORKEEPER

'The doorkeeper is not merely a man to see that each patron has a ticket. He is handy if the box office clerk needs help, he has an eye on the lobby, and he can make patrons feel that they are welcome. If the police regulations permit it is a good plan to have your doorkeeper sworn in as a special constable, picking out a man who is able to handle any trouble that may come his way. The badge represents authority and many who would enjoy a scrap with a doorman will respect the badge.'

How To Run A Picture Theatre, 1911

rushing out. 'Come quickly,' she said, 'a riot is about to break out.'

I shot back inside just in time to see the big man making his way up the aisle shouting, 'Shut up! I've come here to watch the film and you are not swearing in front of my wife.'

The little man was high on something and had been shouting out all evening.

'Hold it,' I said. 'He's got to be got out. I'll fetch the police.'

'I am the police,' said the big man, 'this is my night off.'

At this, the two women sitting on either side of the little man jumped up and went into the attack.

'Police harassment,' they cried. 'Police brutality!'

As if to do his bit, the man who had started it all on this signal began to shout, 'I don't care, slap me again. Go on, slap me again.'

The situation was saved by the appearance of a Sheffield wrestler.

The night President Kennedy was shot, the manager came onto the stage and explained that although they were not stopping the film he would appreciate it if people filed out quietly at the end. I bet they didn't do that the night someone took a shot at Ronald Reagan.

During the Sheffield Blitz on 12 December 1940, when the Moor was destroyed and a lot of people were killed, the manager of one of the picture houses had the lights put up, walked to the front of the stage and said, 'It's a bit lively out there. I'd stay put if I were you'.

Fire drill was another duty. Unfortunately, we weren't told how to differentiate between cigarette and any other kind of smoke.

One thing struck fear into the mind of every cinema manager - fire. Although we maintained all the necessary fire fighting equipment in good order, being checked at intervals by the local Fire Brigade, there was always the thought of how would we cope if there was a fire when we had a full house of over a thousand patrons? We were not allowed to have anything obstructing an exit under penalty of losing the cinema licence and the carpets were examined weekly to make sure there was no risk from tripping over a hole worn in the carpet.

When the phone went and the voice said that a bomb had been placed in the cinema as a reprisal for our part in the Gulf War I knew what to do. I phoned the police and went round the cinema.

'Is there a Mr A Lert in here?' I asked.

'You what?' said the usherette.

'Is there a Mr A ?... Oh, don't bother. It's a bomb.'

'Bloody hell!'

I went to the front, had the lights put up and then said,

'Due to matters beyond our control, the management requests the audience to vacate the cinema quietly.'

No one moved. I must have looked a sight, I was seven months pregnant. In the end I just shouted, 'Out!'

Outside the audience just stood in a crowd around the main entrance. They stood around like sheep waiting to be dipped.

They only responded when tens of firemen in full rig and with breathing apparatus, to the accompaniment of sirens and flashing lights, came rushing up the escalators from the underground car park.

It had got through to them at last that this might be something to do with a bomb. They disappeared like the mist.

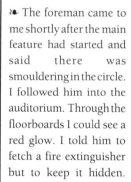If a fire was discovered, the word would be circulated to all staff, who would stand by all exits, and a red spot would appear on the screen. The film would be stopped and the manager would announce a technical breakdown and ask the patrons to leave in an orderly manner. All the exits would be opened and the staff would quietly urge everyone to leave. To encourage people to move along, a brisk march would be played.

The foreman came to me shortly after the main feature had started and said there was smouldering in the circle. I followed him into the auditorium. Through the floorboards I could see a red glow. I told him to fetch a fire extinguisher but to keep it hidden. Meanwhile, I asked people seated nearby to follow me and I led them to the opposite side of the circle. I then went back to the foreman. and stood in front of him as he gently played the jet of water onto the fire. In next to no time it was extinguished. I then allowed patrons back to their seats. I'm certain no-one was any the wiser. It proved to me that it is possible to manipulate a crowd if there is no sense of panic and that most people are prepared to do exactly as they are asked.

I told the organist about the incident and, in tribute, during the interval, he played *I Don't Want To Set The World On Fire*.

In the days of silent films you could always tell the status of a cinema by the type of music that was played. The very best cinemas had an orchestra of at least twenty players and an orchestra pit. The lower class of picture house made do with just a pianist. When sound came along, all of the musicians were out of a job. Except for the pianists, that is. In the early days of talkies the sound often broke down and it was useful to have a pianist on hand - just in case. The ideal arrangement was to employ an usherette who could also play the piano a bit. That meant that you only had to pay a few shillings extra each week.

THE PIANIST

'Get a good one - the best you can afford. This does not mean a concert pianist, for such a player would be worse than useless, and for the same reason do not get one of those who want to show off at the expense of the pictures. Hire someone to play the pictures, and the patient plodder with a fair technique will sometimes be found to be better than a brilliant performer who has a soul above the pictures, and who is continually boasting that Paderewski and De Pachmann are not the only great artistes.'

How To Run A Picture Theatre, 1911

There used to be a pianist at our local cinema who was blind. Everyone knew him as 'Dai the Blind'. He used to have a young boy who sat next to him on the piano stool. This boy would act as Dai's eyes, telling him what was happening on screen so that he could play the appropriate music. This arrangement normally worked very well but I remember one occasion when Dai must have mis-heard the boy because in the middle of a religious film - I think it was *King Of Kings* - Dai threw himself into a rousing chorus of *Here Comes The Galloping Major*.

The organist's programme would often be centred around a theme. If the theme was gardens you would have slides of flowers and tunes such as Kettelby's *In A Chinese Temple Garden* or *In An English Country Garden*.

Naturally, there was community singing. The song slides would be projected onto the screen and a light dot would bounce along the lines to show you where you were.

Ș George was a competent organist and very often enhanced the show by playing popular tunes of the day or the incidental music of forthcoming attractions. On many occasions he would play special requests for patrons who wished to celebrate some anniversary. He always looked smart in his white tuxedo with bow tie and would often produce short programmes in conjunction with the chief operator who manipulated the holophane organ lighting. The organ would be blue as *Blue Skies* was being played, turning to purple with the tune, *Deep Purple*, red for *I Don't Want To Set The World On Fire* and yellow with *Sunny Side Of The Street*.

Ș When I could see that we would be slow to come out of the recession and that the building trade would be particularly badly hit I decided to devote myself to expanding my hobby. I said to myself, 'What do you want at sixty-five?'. And the answer was; 'A cinema'. Instead of just tinkering about with film, I would build myself the real thing and show old movies to my friends. I decided to use my name in the title. Its called *The Ray Olto*.

I had most the skills needed and a lot of the materials required. The mahogany panelling is old school work benches, the wall lighting came from a car boot sale and the seats are genuine. The wallpaper, at £36 a roll, is the most expensive.

It's up and running now. In the entrance there is a proper ticket office so that I can provide special tickets - little mementoes of the visit, really. There's a display of old equipment set out as if you are looking into a supplier's shop. You see all that before going into the cinema proper.

The seating capacity is sixteen and there is wheelchair access - but I've had thirty. It's heated by calor gas but well ventilated so there are no body smells.

On special occasions my wife comes in with little tubs of ice cream and, although it is a bit incongruous, gives out tea and coffee in our best china cups.

Why not come and bring some friends? I've just bought Arthur Askey, Jerry Desmond and Anthea Askey in a film in which Arthur plays a publican in Pontefract. You'll love it.

Ș I didn't go to the pictures with my dad much but there we were in the centre of a crowded circle eating ice cream. Suddenly this beautiful electric organ - a Wurlitzer or a Compton - all flashing lights, cream with gold piping, rose up slowly out of the bowels of the earth. On it sat a man with sleeked-back hair who kept turning and grinning across his shoulder. 'Yon,' said my dad, pointing with his finger, 'is a child molester.'

PROGRAM AND CHOCOLATE SELLERS

'There is no need to enumerate or enlarge upon the duties of the chocolate and program sellers, except to urge that the vending of their wares shall not be too stentorian, for nothing detracts more from the pleasure of patrons than to have a loud voiced boy or girl continually bawling in one's ears 'Chocolates' or 'Programs'.

How To Run A Picture Theatre, 1911

Ș In the interval between features the organ would rise up out of the orchestra pit and the audience was treated to several popular tunes, the first of which was *A Pretty Girl Is Like A Melody*. On this cue, Rhoda and I, dressed in our white coats and hats, set off on our right foot and made our way down each side aisle to the front of the cinema where we turned and gave out with a dazzling smile as the spotlight framed us.

Neither of us was pretty and we both hated this duty. I expect I reacted to a dare. I can't think of any other reason for blacking out my front teeth. At the same time I crossed my eyes. I did this as the spotlight hit me. The audience was enchanted. I sold out of ice cream twice during that duty.

The cinema was a club specialising in blue movies which ran with a skeleton staff. There was me, the cashier and the manageress - all women. The strange thing about the work was that it lacked all the normal things that make working in a cinema enjoyable. The customers never spoke after paying, there was no friendly banter. You just sat there by the door collecting the tickets. Also, there was no trouble - what trouble could you expect from a group of men from the older end, sitting a distance from each other in a dark room watching people grunt at each other?

Fortunately, the manageress didn't insist that we went in to watch the films.

At the Unit Four, Shipley they used to list the first three films, *Jaws, Towering Inferno, The Exorcist* but never bothered with the final unit. They just put up 'Two Sex Films.'

The girl who sold the ice cream in the intervals was a girlfriend of the man up in the projection box who operated the spotlight. She stood at the side of the front of the stage and, when her spot was announced, she would walk slowly across to the other side. But one day she and her man fell out. So, when he shone the spotlight he kept it just in front of her. Hard as she tried, she just couldn't get into its beam.

Saturdays were busy times. One time I took a chap to a seat on the front row in the stalls. 'I want to see the film, not smell it,' he said.

'There's only one other seat available,' I replied, 'at the side of the organist.'

Oh, well, you couldn't please them all.

SEX FILMS

As soon as cinematography emerged as a form of public entertainment films were made which treated sex and nudity as their subject.

As early as 1897 *Photograms of the Year* observed : 'Kinematography has hardly claimed, and certainly has not been recognised as having any artistic pretensions, and yet it has revived, in a very practical manner, the old question of how far the public execution of the nude is admissable. The question arose out of certain subjects published by Philipp Wolff, of Paris, Berlin, and London. In one of them, at least, separate subjects are such as would be accepted at an exhibition of paintings, calmly viewed by all classes of society, and reproduced in our strictly moral illustrated weeklies. But when the subjects are projected in rapid succession, giving a certain illusion of life, their eligibility for public exhibition becomes very doubtful...though when first introduced there was no sale for these subjects in this country, there is now a very brisk and considerable demand. And it may be said for them that they are technically, and even artistically, immensely superior to the bulk of kinetograms on sale.'

Produced mainly in France, these early sex films had titles such as *The Artist's Model, A Bride Unrobing*, and *A French Lady's Bath*. In Britain they were distributed by firms such as Philipp Wolff, motto, 'First Class Shows Only', and the Warwick Trading Company, who described them as 'welcome at any smoking concert or stag party'.

❧ I loved my job as a cinema usherette. Being a movie fan it was a cheap way of seeing all the top films. Not only did I enjoy the work, I really liked wearing the uniform which went with it. It was really something - deep burgundy in colour with gold braid epaulettes and buttons on the made-to-measure coat. The sleeves and lapels were also trimmed with gold braid. At the front we wore a white dickie with a small black bow. Very military looking and, oh, so very smart.

❧ Most cinemas had regulars. We never had an old lady who saw *The Sound Of Music* two hundred times and eventually got presented with the seat but we did have people who saw everything and wouldn't let anyone sit in their seat.

❧ Courting couples were a big topic of discussion amongst usherettes. Some of them must have been contortionists. My sex education was learnt there. To this day any man with a rain coat is suspect.

❧ The stars appearing at the Bradford Alhambra Theatre were given complimentary tickets to see a film. One afternoon during the week I was on duty in the circle when the comedy duo Jimmy Jewel and Ben Wariss came in. Ben Warriss was talking rather loudly. I asked him to 'Shush!' He didn't seem too pleased.

Later, as I checked, I saw that he had his feet on the seat in front. I flashed my torch and asked him to remove them.

'Do you know who I am?' he asked.

'Yes, and you should know better,' I replied.

He glared hard at me, then a smile spread across his face. He put his hand in his pocked and offered me half-a-crown. I refused it.

Fond memories still linger of those days. Now, when I see a film on television that I know by heart, I am back in my uniform, flashing my torch - 'Move along there please and make a double', standing in the spotlight with my ice cream tray - 'Vanilla and choc-ices, orange squash. Sixpence each.'

I suppose that in my own way I'm a show business great!